Dedication

With deep respect and love, I dedicate
this story to the memory of my mother,
Bertha Marie Limbourne, to my stepfather,
Chester W. Limbourne, a man whom mere
words could never describe, and to my
husband, Paul Anthony Brown, who, more
than anyone I have ever known, personifies
personal strength tempered with charity.

It Is I Who
Have Chosen
You

An Autobiography by

JUDIE
BROWN

American Life League
1992

Book Design by Esperanza C. Stewart

Chapter Photography by Stan Beason

Published by American Life League, Inc.

Printed by Anthony Kane & Associates, Inc.

Printed in the United States of America

Table of Contents

Prologue

It is not in my nature to write about myself. I believe sincerely that I am nothing more than God's servant, and that I could accomplish nothing apart from his grace.

Yet I am also aware that each of us, as children of God, has a special mission in life, and that most of us need to be periodically refreshed in our awareness of that awesome truth. So I offer this account of my pilgrimage to date, in the hope that you may see-- even in a life as ordinary as my own--that there is no aspect of life that is without purpose in God's plan. If we will allow the Lord to work through us, tremendous things can happen. Each day is a promise from God that life, while we have it, need never be wasted.

Walk with me, then, through the past forty-eight years. Laugh with me, cry with me, celebrate with me, and mourn with me. See, if you will, the mystery of faith that continues to propel me even now: often beyond my understanding, sometimes even against my will, but always with the trust that in God everything has a purpose.

I am not suggesting that my life is a road map or model for others to follow. It surely is not. It is, however, a simple story of a simple woman who has come to know the value of faith, and who has seen the Lord work because of it.

In the gospel of John we learn of our union with Christ and how it comes about. Jesus says:

> You are my friends if you do the things I command you. No longer do I call you servants, because the servant does not know what his master does. But I have called you friends, because all things that I have heard from my Father I have made known to you. You have not chosen me, it is I who have chosen you (John 15:14-16).

A Mother's Love: No Matter What!

1944 - 1952

In him who is
the source
of my
strength, I
have
strength for
everything.

Philippians 4:13

Chapter One

AS MY MOTHER never tired of pointing out, I entered the world a difficult and obstinate person. I was a "breech" baby, meaning that I was trying to come out of the birth canal backwards. The doctors had to turn me around before I could be born. Even while I was still in the womb, I was giving others a challenge! Some things, my mother would say, never change.

This was in March, 1944. My mother had been married to my father for a little over a year. It was only eighteen months later that my sister Sheila was born. Though I was too young to remember it, it was then that my life changed radically.

My father deserted us.

While my mother was still in Our Lady of Angels Hospital in Los Angeles recovering from Sheila's birth, my father had other fish to fry with a woman who took up the time that should have gone to his wife and family. Within a week of Sheila's birth, he was gone from our lives forever.

As it turned out, my mother had been his fifth wife—a fact she never knew.

That pain was intense at the time my father left. Mama's selfless love had been betrayed. Now she was left with two small babies, and nowhere to go.

In later years my grandmother—Mama's mother, Bertha Teckla Baldi—told me how worried she was about my mother during this time. For months after the divorce Mama wept in anguish. She never let my sister or me see that side of her, though. She suffered in private. It was almost a year before she was able to start putting her life, and ours, back together again.

Ultimately we moved in with Grandma and Grandpa Baldi. They opened their hearts, and their modest home on Harcourt

Avenue in Los Angeles, to the three of us. They made life as joyful for Mama as they could, always realizing that her dreams of home and family might be dashed forever.

How well I remember those years! Mama would leave for work each morning, leaving Sheila and me under the care of our doting grandparents. Grandpa worked as a bricklayer—when there was work to be found. When there wasn't, he would stay home and help look after us. He would play with us and talk with us, smoking his cigar and blowing big smoke rings in the air. He was cheerful and playful—until we did something to make Grandma upset. Then he got more than a little irritated with us.

This often happened when Grandma braided our hair. We would scream, yell at her, and call her names. She would become exasperated, bop us on the head with the brush, and call Grandpa in for reinforcement. We would end up in chairs in opposite corners of the dining room. But we never learned: the next time Grandma tried to braid our hair, we raised Cain all over again.

Right: Bertha Tekla Schreck, my maternal grandmother, at her wedding to Louis W. Baldi; Harry and Elsie are behind them.

Below: Grandma Baldi in 1951.

Grandma and Grandpa, like all good Germans, believed in orderliness and obedience. The rules they set for us, and the standards of behavior to which they held us, were unbending. That doesn't mean that Sheila and I were especially orderly or obedient, however. We knew there would be consequences when we crossed the line. But we never let that stop us from crossing it anyway!

For example, Grandpa did not want us to take food to our room. But Sheila and I had other ideas, and became very adept at crawling under the bed covers with cookies, milk, candy, chips, and other goodies we had smuggled out of the kitchen. Of course there was always incriminating evidence later on: crumbs, spills, and wrappers that we had left behind. But even being caught and punished didn't seem to spoil our desire to simply do it again the next night.

One of our favorite activities was helping Grandma with the

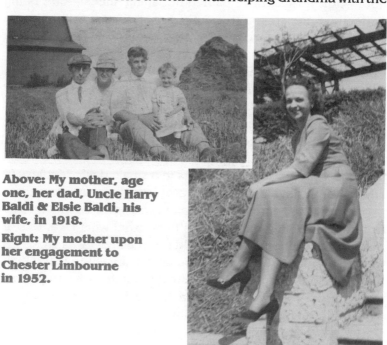

Above: My mother, age one, her dad, Uncle Harry Baldi & Elsie Baldi, his wife, in 1918.

Right: My mother upon her engagement to Chester Limbourne in 1952.

laundry. She had one of those old-fashioned washing machines with a wringer. One day Sheila and I decided we could
somehow speed up the process by sticking our hands into the
tub and helping move the clothes around. You guessed it: I got
my arm caught in the wringer. I screamed, Sheila screamed,
and Grandma had a fit. After she freed my arm, I had the nerve
to blame her for what had happened!

Not all my childhood experiences had to do with being
naughty, though. I especially remember Wednesday nights,
when I would go with Grandma to the weekly Rosary. We'd
leave the house right after dinner and walk around the corner
to the home of a neighbor lady. In her living room were a vigil
candle and a beautiful statue of Our Lady crushing the head of
the serpent. I remember kneeling next to Grandma on the hard
floor—how it must have pained her aging knees!—and being
perfectly content to pray the entire Rosary. As we walked home
I would ask why we couldn't go more often. I remember the
smile on my mother's face when we got home. She could see
that praying with Grandma was something I really loved to do.

Grandma and Grandpa loved us, and were only too happy
to do things to please us. Sheila and I quickly learned to exploit
their generous natures. Whenever the ice cream man came
down our street, we could always rely on one or the other (or
both) of them to treat us to a popsicle. Sometimes we were able
to orchestrate three or four treats in a single day! Needless to
say, we both developed weight problems from an early age.

By the time I entered first grade at St. John's school, I was
accomplished at manipulating others to get what I wanted. If
I wanted to go home early, I told the teacher I was sick. If I
wanted attention, I claimed to be having an asthma attack. If
I complained loud enough and long enough, I always got my
way. Except for the asthma attacks—at least some of which
were quite real—Sheila could play all the same cards.

I shudder to think what sort of children we would have
become had it not been for the man who entered Mama's life
at about this time.

A Father for All Seasons

1953 - 1957

Husbands should love their wives as they do their own bodies. He who loves his wife loves himself. Observe that no one ever hates his own flesh; no, he nourishes it and takes care of it as Christ cares for the church—for we are members of his body.

Ephesians 5:28-29

Chapter Two

MAMA WAS STILL YOUNG, and quite attractive, and she had two younger brothers who were not unaware of those facts. It seemed they were always bringing someone home to meet her. I remember some of those fellows, and—to be quite frank—I'm thankful Mama had the good taste to pass on them.

All but one, that is.

Chester Limbourne came to know my mother through Uncle George, Mama's baby brother. I remember the first time Chester came to the house. I remember him coming many other times, taking Mama out for the evening. And I especially remember the night Mama talked to Grandma about getting married again. Or, at first, about not getting married again.

Needless to say, our mother's marital status was a topic of great interest to Sheila and me, so we had our ears pressed to the door as Mama explained to Grandma why she felt she could not accept Chester Limbourne's proposal of marriage—even though she thought him the most wonderful man in the world.

Mama was thirty-four at the time, and she suffered from rheumatoid arthritis in her legs and arms. She had to go to downtown Los Angeles for "gold treatments" at City of Hope Hospital on a regular basis. She was afraid that her arthritis, plus the fact that she had two children, would simply be too much for Chester to handle.

Sheila and I were horrified. We didn't know much about the world at that age, but we knew that we thought Chester Limbourne was terrific. He always gave us a big hug when he came for Mama, and he was so nice to Grandma and Grandpa. We were happy to see Mama with someone who was so nice, and we couldn't believe she'd pass up an opportunity to marry him.

Chester finally got over all Mama's objections by focusing on the one thing that made marriage the right decision for her: he simply loved her more than anything else in the world, and he wanted more than anything to be her husband and our father.

From the moment they walked down the aisle, Sheila and I knew that we had a real father, someone who loved our mother and us, someone who cared about the security of our little family. Though we were not bone of his bone and flesh of his flesh, he always treated us as though we were. The sacrifices he made for us would require another book to recount.

And so, in 1951, we moved into a house of our own. Sheila and I had never seen Mama so happy. We almost didn't know what to make of it! But we never questioned that life was wonderful.

Our little family was soon blessed by two additions. A brother, Mark, was born in 1952. Two years later my sister Ann arrived. The babies were the center of attention. I loved taking care of them for my mother, who was still bothered by her arthritis.

Mark required special care, because he was a special baby: he was born with Down's Syndrome. He seldom cried—in fact, it seemed as though he always had a smile on his face—and whenever he became ill, Mama became very anxious.

And with good reason. Mark's immune system was under-developed, which meant that even the slightest sniffle could swiftly develop into a form of pneumonia. Every one of us did our best to protect him from germs, but from time to time he would catch cold and have to be nursed around the clock. When that happened, Mama, Sheila, and I had to team up. Mama would handle the night shift, and Sheila and I would take turns staying home from school so we could care for Mark during the day, while Mama slept.

In the fall of 1954, when he was two-and-a-half years old, Mark came down with one of his occasional colds. But this time was different. He fell more gravely ill than he ever had before.

He didn't respond to being touched. He was in a state of sleepiness from which he never seemed to completely awaken.

I came home from school one afternoon to find Mama in a panic. She was on the phone with the doctor. Before I knew it we were out the door, in the car, racing to the hospital. I sat next to Mama in the front seat, holding Mark in my lap. He was so weak he was barely breathing. It was a fifteen-minute ride to the hospital. Mark didn't make it. He died in my arms.

I'll never forget that awful afternoon. Daddy met us at the hospital. So did the doctor, who coldly pronounced Mark dead, and then had the gall to tell us that we were all probably "better off."

Looking back, I'm sure my mother always knew that Mark's condition was such that he could not survive to adulthood. But her faith enabled her to use each moment she spent caring for him as a testimony to her confidence that God would look after her son. She and Daddy always treated Mark and Ann as though they were equal, even though Mark was never able to walk or even to crawl. We used to sit together on Sunday evenings and watch the Walt Disney program. We all enjoyed it, but Mark enjoyed it more than anyone. Just hearing the theme song made him giggle and bounce up and down. Indeed, all music affected him that way: it made him happy.

We went through the next few days after Mark's death as if in a trance. Friends and family members flocked to our aid at once. Though each one offered loving sympathy, the loss was simply too much for my mother to bear. Against all reason, she blamed herself for what had happened. Wanting to be alone in her grief, she shut out everyone except Daddy—who was, as always, her rock, her fortress, her friend.

Things only got tougher for Mama as the year went on. Her arthritis hit her harder than ever. She developed bleeding ulcers. She was hospitalized a couple of times. With each setback, Daddy grew stronger, more compassionate, more in love with this woman who was suffering so.

He also grew more demanding of the rest of us, to be patient with Mama, to love her, to avoid doing things that would upset her. Of course, all children hear their fathers scold them, "Don't upset your mother!" But I always felt that Daddy spoke more from a genuine concern for her well-being than from a simple desire to keep us in line. He loved her so much that he suffered with her, though he never suggested that her difficulties were weighing him down.

I still remember the small but beautifully decorated Christmas tree we placed at Mark's grave the year he died. I also remember Mama's tears as we placed the tree by his grave marker. It became an annual trip for us, and each time we felt the loss as keenly as though Mark had just left us the day before.

I see now that the aftermath of Mark's death was so severe precisely because of the unselfish love my parents had for him while he was alive. Had they cared less about him while he was alive, they would have cared less about his death. But from the moment he was born, when they rejected the doctor's suggestion that they put Mark in a home somewhere because he could never lead a "normal" life, my parents loved Mark as deeply as they loved all the rest of us.

Maybe it is fair to say they loved him even more, because his needs were so much greater. He required long, hard hours of care, which they surely would rather have spent doing something else; but they never stinted. He needed to be at home virtually all the time, which many would find inconvenient; but they never complained. There was simply nothing they would not have done for their son, while at the same time making sure that my sisters and I never felt left out.

Looking back on this hectic period, I cannot help but wonder how Daddy coped with the powerful emotions that must have welled up inside him. Mama's rapid deterioration meant he never really had time to mourn the death of his only son. I wonder how many other men would have handled it the way he did, always placing his wife's needs first? I was too young to appreciate what he was going through, or the grace with which he handled it.

I only know that no words can do justice to his role in our family through those dark days. Is it any wonder that I consider Chester Limbourne such a great man?

Going to K-Mart

1958 - 1964

I will instruct
you and
show you the
way you
should walk;
I will counsel
you, keeping
my eye on
you.

Psalm 32:8

Chapter Three

GRADUALLY LIFE began to level out. Ann, the baby of the family, turned three. I turned thirteen—a very large thirteen, I might add. I was seriously over-weight. Had I been a boy, I'm sure I could have been a star lineman on the high school football team.

Mama's arthritis seemed to recede a bit. She moved a bit slower than she would have liked, but she managed to do pretty much everything she wanted to do. And she had a lot of things she wanted to do. She served as chauffeur for the nuns at our local grade school, and as head chef for the big weekly dinners we held at our house for all the family—as many as twenty people each week! She prepared baked goods for the church whenever they asked, made most of our clothes, and even held down a part-time job stuffing envelopes and collating materials for a local business. She never complained, never made excuses, never asked for sympathy. She just did what she felt she should do, and made the best of her physical limitations.

Somehow, in spite of all this, she still had the ability to "be there" for us when we needed her. She simply seemed to radiate love to others. Neither Ann, Sheila, nor I ever brought home a "stranger." Everyone was welcome; everyone was made to feel part of the family. In fact, countless numbers of our friends came home with us after school, or dropped in on weekends, just to talk with Mrs. Limbourne, the wonderful lady who always had time to listen, a good word to say, and a warm smile with brown eyes that could cut right through your troubles.

We were just an ordinary family, dealing with the problems that everyone faced in the late 50s. There was a budget that allowed only for short vacations, three young girls who never seemed to stop arguing—all the normal things you might remember (or choose to forget!) about your own childhood.

When I turned sixteen, Daddy decided to take on the job of teaching me to drive. We went to the Hollywood Race Track, in suburban Inglewood, which had a huge parking lot. Daddy figured I'd need plenty of room if I was to avoid endangering the safety of others. And he was right. To this day I cannot parallel-park. I even have trouble backing up. I'm not the person you'd want to have at the wheel in a tight situation.

It was also about this time that I decided to begin a chapter of the Johnny Mathis Fan Club. I answered an ad in a teen magazine from someone in Maine who was looking for help expanding the club. I wrote tons of letters and made hundreds of long-distance phone calls. I finally found myself president of the largest chapter of the entire fan club. I wrote regularly to Johnny Mathis, of course, whom I adored but had never met. I recounted all the details of how the fan club was growing, trusting that he pored over every word I wrote.

Then, one day, the phone rang. It was Johnny Mathis's agent. Johnny was going to be making an appearance soon at the Coconut Grove, and wanted to invite my parents and me to come as his personal guests! After the show, we were invited backstage to meet Johnny in his dressing room. I was in heaven!

Looking back, I marvel at my parents' patience through all this. They never told me I was being a silly teenage girl, never even complained about the cost of all those letters and phone

Left: Me, four months. Center: Me, two years. Right: Me, age six, first grade.

Lower left: Me in Mexico, 1953. Lower right: Me and my sister Sheila, 1953.

calls. They just supported me in what I wanted to do, believing that children were better served if they had wholesome activities that helped them understand the ways of the world.

They sacrificed for us in so many ways: music lessons twice a week for ten years; new clothes when we simply "had to have them," an excellent (and expensive) education at the parish school. When I think of the many things they must have had to do without, I'm saddened by the fact that as a child I never appreciated, let alone thanked them for, all that they did for me. If anything, I only grew more demanding, and more outspoken when I didn't get my way. It took me a long time to learn what Daddy so often told me: "Money doesn't grow on trees, Judie!"

But I began to learn the value of a dollar when I started taking various part-time jobs. I delivered Fuller Brush products for a local salesman. I taught beginning accordion at the studio where I myself took lessons. I filled in behind the jewelry counter of the nearby Kresge's five-and-dime. None of these jobs demanded a great deal of time, but they did begin to teach me the importance of commitment and hard work.

I also volunteered as a "Candy Striper," or nurse's aide, at the local hospital. I was easily bored, and needed lots of activities to keep me busy. Working in the hospital didn't bring in any money, but it taught me some important lessons. It cemented a lesson I had learned from the way we had cared for Mark: that those who are suffering are the ones for whom we must make time. I still remember the faces of patients who would see me and know that I would always stop and talk with them for a while, even if they were not going to buy one of my candy bars or packages of Kleenex. My grandfather lived right across the street from the hospital—he had moved there after Grandma died—and I would visit him, too, cleaning up the apartment or just chatting.

As high school graduation approached, the time came to settle on some more stable plans for the future. I knew I wanted to go to college, and at first I thought I wanted to be a child psychologist. I had good grades and was accepted at every college I applied to. I was even offered a full scholarship at New

York University. But I turned it down because I realized my career goals were not sufficiently well-planned to leave my family and go three thousand miles away. My parents were thrilled by the honor of my being offered the scholarship—and relieved, I think, when I decided not to accept it.

I weighed all my options and discussed things at length with my parents. We talked a lot about the medical profession, with which I was so enamored. Mama was afraid that my inclination to become personally involved with anyone who had a problem might be my undoing. I had to agree.

We finally determined that the business world provided the best fit for my talents. So I stayed at home, stayed on at the local Kresge's—I had by now become bookkeeper for the entire store—and registered for the fall semester at a local college.

A year later I decided it was time to move out and live on my own. I took an apartment just a few blocks from my parents' house. Not long after, my father finalized a decision he had been contemplating for some time: the family would move away. My baby sister, Ann, was now eight years old, and Daddy wanted her to have a horse and a big yard and the kind of environment that southern California could no longer provide. And so, in the summer of 1963, Mama and Daddy and Sheila and Ann packed up and moved to Oregon, while I remained in Los Angeles.

My career was developing nicely. Within a few months I had been promoted from the local store to the western regional headquarters of what was now known as the K-Mart Corporation. I continued my studies, worked under a couple of brilliant corporate vice presidents, and within a year was invited to become the western regional office manager—a position that had never before been offered to a woman of only twenty-one.

After consulting with my family, I accepted the promotion. It meant a lot of travel, and discontinuing my education, but it seemed like the right step. I began criss-crossing the eleven states in K-Mart's western region, overseeing training for new stores, and meeting people who were in upper-level management positions with the company.

One of these was a very interesting man named Paul Brown.

Romancing the Blarney Stone

1964 - 1967

Love never fails.
There are in the
end three things
that last: faith,
hope and love,
and the greatest
of these is love.

1 Corinthians 13:13

Chapter Four

TRAVELLING AROUND the western United States in the early 1960s was a great job for a young woman. I had freedom, I had a good salary, and I had the responsibilities of an executive and the perks that went with them.

Frankly, it has always been a bit hard for me to understand it when I hear women complain about the difficulties of competing in the job world. I can honestly say I never faced any sort of discrimination. I worked hard, I did my job well, and I was recognized and rewarded for it. What has changed since those days? Has the business world suddenly turned against talent and hard work? Or have women begun trying to imitate or replace men, rather than complement and support them? In any case, my own corporate adventure was wonderful.

One of my first assignments, in the fall of 1964, was to help open a new store in Ogden, Utah. This particular store had special importance to the company: it was going to pioneer a new design. An experienced manager, a Mr. Paul A. Brown, had been assigned to oversee the opening, and to make sure that the layout of the store was perfect, right down to the last tube of toothpaste.

Mr. Brown, I was told, was bright, energetic, and experienced. There was just one problem. For some reason, he absolutely refused to punch in and out on his time card. Yet he insisted on being paid overtime. Since part of my job was to serve as supervisor of payroll, one of my first tasks was to set Mr. Brown straight.

I went looking for him one Thursday afternoon as my staff was trying to complete the week's payroll. I found him squatting down in front of a display case, arranging merchandise on the bottom shelf.

"Mr. Brown?" I asked.

He didn't even look up. "Yeah," he muttered.

"Mr. Paul A. Brown?" I asked, using my most intimidating supervisory tone of voice.

Now he looked up. "What do you want?" he snapped.

"It's about your overtime," I said. "You haven't been punching in your time card, and I can't pay you until you do."

"Go to h___."

Well! I stood over him, all 210 pounds of me, and gave him a stern lecture on K-Mart company policy. The company would not allow me to pay his overtime, I said, even though he was on salary, if he did not record the hours. The company was most generous with managers like himself, I said, but the company also needed a record, so . . .

He didn't say anything. He just stood up, glared at me for a second, then shook his head and walked away. As far as I know, he never did punch a time card—he probably felt it was too demeaning for a manager—and he never got paid for his overtime.

I, of course, was speechless with anger. Nobody was going to talk to Judie Limbourne like that! For the next three years, whenever our paths crossed, I always found some way to insert a snide remark or otherwise express my dislike for him.

So you can imagine my reaction when a friend suggested, some three years later, that I call a halt to the feud. It was embarrassing to the company, she said, and it couldn't possibly be doing my career any good. Besides, she said, Paul Brown was really a warm, friendly person, and she was sure I'd like him if I would only give him a chance.

Well, why not? I thought. It had been three years, after all; a lot of water had flowed over the dam. I had advanced in position and salary. I had lost eighty pounds. I was driving a Lincoln Continental, which I thought was pretty good for a twenty-three-year-old woman. And the store he now managed was only an hour's drive away, in Bellevue, Washington. So, one Wednesday afternoon, I drove the fifty miles to Bellevue and dropped in on my old nemesis.

Mr. Brown was extraordinarily polite. We chatted about the

"business" I had come to discuss, then he walked me to my car. Before I drove off, he asked if he could call me. I said yes.

That was how our relationship started. In the coming weeks we had several dates, a number of long conversations, and more than a few stormy disagreements.

One date was especially memorable. We were going out to dinner with a couple whom Paul had known since childhood. The man had retired from the military, and had invited us to be his guests at the officers' club at Sandy Point naval base on Puget Sound. It was lovely and romantic. Music flowed from a juke box in the corner, and Paul and I danced for hours. Finally, while Frank Sinatra sang "Strangers in the Night," Paul asked me to marry him.

I did what any love-struck twenty-three-year-old would have done under the circumstances. I laughed at him.

I hadn't known him all that long, but I knew him well enough to know that he had a full complement of Irish mischief in his personality. The proposal, I was sure, was just part and parcel of

Paul and I dating, 1967.

the Paul A. Brown mystique—another bit of blarney. So I laughed.

But when Paul asked me again, and I could see in his eyes that he was sincere, I didn't laugh any more. I just looked back at him and said, "Yes."

Many people have been astounded by how brief our courtship was. I must admit, sometimes I myself have looked back on it in wonderment. But both Paul and I somehow knew from the start that we were like a hand in a glove: made for each other. I truly believe that God had his hand on us from the beginning. In any case, over the next few weeks we had several serious conversations, which convinced me beyond a doubt that there was no one else in the entire world with whom I would rather spend the rest of my life. I knew I now had two of the most wonderful men in the world deeply involved in my life.

I couldn't wait to tell my mother. She was my confidante, the only person I trusted with my deepest feelings, my fears, my dreams, the cares of my heart and soul. She was always a good listener and a wise counselor, a beacon of light in the darkness. Whenever I had something important to talk about, I always relied on her guidance and advice.

Right: My engagement photo.

Below: Walking down the aisle with Daddy.

So when I called to tell her that Paul and I were engaged and planning to be married that December, I was eager to hear her response.

"Judie," she said at once, "this will never last. You haven't known him long enough."

As we talked, I understood her reservations more clearly. She had only met Paul once before, when I had brought him home for a weekend, and she had been less than impressed. For some reason Paul had been quiet around the family, almost withdrawn. Perhaps he was nervous, meeting the people he was planning to have as his in-laws. Perhaps he was just put off by the (admittedly) goofy sense of humor that prevailed in our home. In any case, he had not been himself, and my mother had come away convinced that he was not the man for me.

Even so, Mama respected my ability to make decisions for myself, and she was happy to see me so happy. In the end, she gave us her blessing.

The engagement was brief and occasionally stormy. My parents had the wedding announcements printed and in the mail when Paul and I had a huge argument one night and called off the whole thing. When I told Mama, she took it in stride. The

The wedding party, December 30, 1967.

cancellation notices, she assured me, could be in the mail within seventy-two hours. Fortunately it took Paul and me only forty-eight hours to make up, and the wedding was on again. Everything moved along peacefully from that point onward.

Barely three months after that magical evening at the naval base, Paul and I were married at the same church in Hawthorne, California, where I had received my first Holy Communion as a little girl. The wedding had been planned long distance: my parents had moved back to California a few years before, and my mother's health had begun to deteriorate again, so I handled as many of the details as I could from Washington, where I was working.

I remember every detail of that day, much as I am sure you remember your own wedding day. The flowers were perfect, the church was magnificent, the priest was magnanimous, and magic filled the air. I remember wishing that my grandparents could have been there, as I knew they would have been pleased. I wished that my mother could have been completely healthy.

But most of all I remember my parents and the joy they exuded. Paul, who was proving to be one of the most complex and intriguing people I had ever known, had by now managed to endear himself to my family, and they couldn't have been happier for us. These two people had given so much and sacrificed so selflessly, not only for me but also for my sisters. Now they watched me begin a new family, which I would always hope to model after the lessons I had learned in my own childhood. Their tears of joy were part of what made that day so perfect.

After a honeymoon in San Francisco, Paul and I set up housekeeping in a brand-new apartment in Seattle. A whole new phase of life was beginning for this obstinate woman of German descent and this marvelous man who reflected every characteristic that the Irish are famous for, from his grand sense of humor to his total dedication to family.

New Baby,
New Battle

1968 - 1970

The Lord keeps faith; he it is who will strengthen you and guard you against the evil one.

2 Thessalonians 3:3

Chapter Five

MY FIRST OFFICIAL ACTION as Mrs. Paul A. Brown was to resign my position with K-Mart. The job still required a lot of travel, and Paul and I felt that wouldn't be good for our marriage. Paul himself had left the company a month before our wedding, because the prospect of relocating every six to eight months—not uncommon for those on the management track—seemed too disruptive. Besides, we had both grown attached to the Seattle area.

I took a job with the now-defunct White Front stores, a chain of discount retail outlets not dissimilar to K-Mart. I was head bookkeeper for their store in Tacoma. Paul entered management training with White Front, overseeing a store in Seattle. The two stores were thirteen miles apart. We bought a small home about halfway between them, adopted a Weimaraner puppy, and began settling into married life.

But not into family life, precisely: we had decided to wait a while before having children. I went to a gynecologist to get a prescription for birth control pills. At this time, neither Paul nor I had any qualms about The Pill; neither of us had been exposed to anything that would suggest that there was anything wrong, either medically or morally, with using it. For us, it was a simple proposition: we didn't want to start a family just yet, and taking The Pill was the most effective way to prevent pregnancy.

There was only one problem.

After examining me, the gynecologist told me that it was a little late to be investigating birth control: I was already six weeks pregnant!

After the initial shock wore off, Paul and I were ecstatic. We picked out colors for the baby's room, began setting aside as much money as we could muster, and shared the good news with anyone who had a telephone. On November 23, 1968, after twelve hours of difficult labor, Hugh Richard Brown III was born. We named him after Paul's father, who had died before Paul and I met. Naturally, Hugh was the most beautiful baby anyone had ever had.

We did all the usual things that new parents do: we bought a crib and toys and a bassinet, we read every book we could get our hands on about what to do when the baby cries, we made faces about the dirty diapers and fumbled with the diaper pins. We did everything except have the baby baptized.

Let me explain. I had been a lukewarm Catholic, at best. Paul, though he had been raised a Catholic, had long since lost interest in it, and for the first two years of our marriage refused to have anything to do with it.

I was a willing accomplice, to be sure, in our decision to ignore Sunday Mass. Paul and I would tell ourselves that Sunday was our only real time to be with the baby, so it made sense to skip church, stay home, and enjoy our little family. I occasionally put up token resistance, and I think Paul and I both knew our thinking was quite selfish. But in the end, when Sunday morning rolled around, we stayed home.

When Hugh was born, the subject of baptism came up

Me, Hugh, age one month, & Baron von Schnell Blitz Brown.

briefly. But Paul vehemently refused even to consider it. He wouldn't have his child baptized into a faith he himself was not practicing. And that was that.

At the same time, because Hugh's birth had been so difficult on me, the doctor was recommending that I use The Pill in order to avoid becoming pregnant again right away.

By now I had read enough about The Pill to have serious misgivings about its health consequences, so I asked if I could use an IUD instead. My doctor, who was a practicing Catholic, approved my request and inserted the device without comment. He never told me that the IUD is, in effect, an abortifacient; he never suggested that I discuss the matter with a priest; he never said one word to me about the matter other than "okay."

This took place in January, 1969. Hugh had been born two months before. Humanae Vitae, the Church's statement on birth control, had been issued eight months before. It is an indication of the state of my Catholicism that I had no idea the Church did not condone any artificial birth control. Nor did anyone ever tell me this was the case. At that stage in my spiritual life, knowing the Church's position might not have mattered to me anyway. In any case, I got the IUD.

While Hugh was still an infant, Paul left White Front and became an insurance salesman. He worked with several different companies before settling in with one of the country's largest and best-known organizations. Almost immediately he became their top salesman.

One weekend Paul was in San Francisco, attending a sales seminar, when he called me late one night. He sounded excited. "Judie," he said, "I want you to make an appointment with the priest at the local parish. I want to go to confession and return to the Church."

I had no idea where this new line of thinking had come from. Perhaps Paul had been rethinking our conversations about baptizing Hugh, or the foolish ways we justified skipping Mass on Sundays. Perhaps someone at the seminar said something that challenged Paul to renew his faith—which, I believe, had never really died but simply gone into "spiritual hibernation." I had no insight at all into the process. I only knew the result: we were going back to church.

Frankly, I was relieved. Despite all the reassurances we gave each other that what we were doing was okay, I knew in my heart that we had turned our backs on the Church—on the Lord—for no reason other than laziness, and I could never shake the nagging thought that if anything were to happen to either of us, we were headed straight for hell.

I had thought on more than one occasion of simply bundling up the baby and going to Mass by myself, but I was afraid Paul would be angry. During those early months and years of marriage, while we were still struggling to adjust to each other, I guess I was insecure enough that I didn't want to provoke any disagreements that might turn into fights that might turn into separation and divorce. Silly, perhaps, but that was what I feared might happen. That, plus a heavy dose of my own lukewarmness, was more than enough to keep me away from church.

But Paul's phone call changed everything. I contacted the pastor, Fr. Willonberg, the very next morning. I explained to him that both Paul and I wanted to come back to church, wanted to make a general confession and receive the sacraments, and wanted to have our son baptized. He didn't bat an eye, God bless him.

Soon all the arrangements were made. We visited Fr. Willonberg and made our confessions. What a feeling of warmth and security! The next Sunday we went to Mass. Hugh, now eighteen months old, was baptized that morning. Not too many babies are able to walk forward to be baptized, wearing a suit, and chatting with the priest all the while, but that's how it was for Hugh. We had called the couple who had hosted us for that fateful dinner at the naval Officers' Club and asked them to be Hugh's godparents. All in all, it was quite a week.

It was also at about this time that I had the IUD removed. Not because of any convictions about either its abortifacient properties or the Church's position on birth control; we were still ignorant on those topics. We had simply decided that we wanted to have more children, and didn't want to wait. I had recovered sufficiently from Hugh's birth that the health risk was largely removed, and I had taken quite well to being a full-time wife and mother. Paul and I decided we wanted six children, and we couldn't wait to get started. By the next summer, Baby Brown number two was on the way.

By this time we were attending Mass regularly. In fact, it was while we were at Mass one Sunday that Fr. Willonberg said something that would turn our lives upside down.

He spoke, with great distress, of a referendum question that was to be on the ballot in Washington state that November. The purpose of the referendum was to liberalize the state's abortion law.

Abortion. In those days the word still had the power to shock people, and it shocked Paul and me that Sunday morning. Here we were, brand-new parents with a baby on the way, newly returned to the faith of our childhoods, hearing a sermon about people who wanted to kill little babies with the full consent of the law. It felt as though the earth had moved under our pew. How, I wondered, could a mother willfully seek the destruction of her own child?

Hugh, at three months.

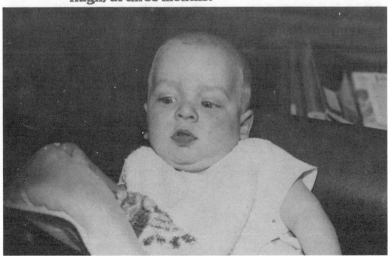

I was soon to find out, however, that there were many women who thought nothing of it; who thought that their own sexual freedom should supersede any other claims; who thought they should have the right to do away with the "problems" created by their own choices and actions.

So when Fr. Willonberg invited us to work with him, distributing pro-life literature door-to-door and asking our neighbors and friends to be sure to vote "no" on Referendum 20, Paul and I were eager to get involved. That was the beginning of our battle to save the little children, like our own, whose lives had begun so simply but with such miraculous heavenly intervention.

Today, years later, people often tell me how inane the arguments of the pro-death forces seem to them. I take no pleasure in telling them that in 1970, in Washington state, the arguments were exactly the same. Then as now, there were people who believed that not all human beings were created equal, and that the law should permit some human beings to murder other human beings when it suited their convenience. People were just as selfish and depraved then as they are now.

The only difference is that then there were no organized pro-life groups ready and willing to fight for the rights of the preborn. Just five months after our rag-tag group began its door-to-door campaign, in a close vote, the people of the state of Washington said yes to abortion.

We were crushed. How could it have happened? Where would it end? How could we stop it?

Blessed Are the Poor

1970 - 1972

I was hard pressed and was
falling, but the Lord helped
 me.
My strength and my courage
is the Lord, and he has been
my savior.

Psalm 118:13-14

Chapter Six

AS IT TURNED OUT, the 1970 referendum defeat in Washington state was far from the only blow our family was to suffer that year. They say that adversity is a great teacher. Well, the Lord chose 1970 to shower us with painful lessons.

That summer, amid the frenetic door-to-door literature campaign, we took a Sunday afternoon off and went to a company picnic. A lot of the dads were taking their kids down an especially high, steep slide on the playground. Paul took Hugh down the slide a couple of times, much to their mutual delight. For some reason, on the third time down they picked up speed more than before. Afraid that he might drop Hugh onto the concrete playground surface, Paul clutched him tightly with both arms and then tried to stop by digging his heels into the hard surface.

The result: a shattered kneecap, several weeks in and out of the hospital, a full leg cast for six months, inability to pursue his career as a salesman, and the sudden realization that although he was the number-one salesman for a major insurance company, he had never sold himself a disability policy!

Because he worked strictly on commission, this meant no income for our family. Here we were with one baby and another on the way, a mortgage, two car payments, a pile of credit card bills, and no way to pay them. What followed was humbling and anguishing—but, in God's master plan, much to our benefit.

I had some unemployment insurance coming to me, which I applied for. Paul received a small check as well. We quickly learned how to survive on twenty dollars a week for groceries. When we fell hopelessly behind with our bills, we filed for bankruptcy and "homesteaded" our house, a legal maneuver that enabled us to stay in our home without bank foreclosure until we could regain a steady income and pay down our debts.

In time, we did exactly that. But the intervening six months were just awful. I am still grateful to our neighbors, who really pitched in and helped us. They understood our predicament and they were there for us. Not once did they speak or act in a way that added to the embarrassment I knew Paul was feeling. And to think it all happened because he tried to take his son down a playground slide one summer afternoon!

Our main form of entertainment was going to the drive-in movie once a week. It was cheap, and it enabled Paul to stretch out his leg in the back seat. Besides, we couldn't afford a baby-sitter, and going to the drive-in made it possible to take Hugh with us.

Paul started to go stir-crazy more than once during that period. The combination of boredom, embarrassment, and frustration was almost more than he could handle. But he never lost his perspective. I was the one who did that! I would burst into tears over what I saw as the hopelessness of our situation. Having worked as a credit manager for so many different stores, the idea of declaring personal bankruptcy was especially galling to me. But Paul would firmly assure me that we would survive, and that we would never experience such an ordeal again, as long as he had anything to say about it.

Paul was still in the midst of his rehabilitation when the second little Brown made her appearance on the scene. And a memorable appearance it was! We were having Sunday brunch at a neighbor's house—I was tucking into a short stack of pancakes with peach preserves—when the first labor pangs hit. Remembering how long the labor process had been with Hugh, I wasn't overly concerned. I casually mentioned to Paul that after breakfast we should probably consider starting off for the hospital.

We very nearly didn't make it. Catherine Marie Brown (named for her two grandmothers) was born just three hours later. Paul was able to be present for the delivery and was the first one to hold her—the nurses cleaned her up and presented her to him with a tiny pink bow in her hair. He was one proud father. "Judie, I was really praying for a girl," he told me. "I'm the youngest of four boys, so I especially wanted a daughter."

Cathy's big brother was also quite enthusiastic upon her arrival home. He could hardly wait to hold her, feed her, give her a bath, and do anything else I was willing to let him try. Actually, life was quite a panic in the Brown household during those first few weeks. Between the new baby, little Hugh—who was only two-and-a-half—and Paul, who was still hobbled by his knee injury, it was hard to keep track of just exactly who was taking care of whom. We even had neighbors dropping in to help Hugh help Paul take care of Cathy so that I could take care of everything else. If you think it sounds confusing, you should have been there to see it!

Two months after Cathy was born I went back to the doctor, and to our pastor, to discuss birth control. The danger still existed with regard to my health. My womb had been seriously weakened during Cathy's delivery, and my body was too weak to withstand another pregnancy any time soon. So, with the blessing of a Catholic priest and a doctor who was also a Catholic, another IUD was inserted.

It astonishes me now, looking back on the experience, that both our priest and our doctor were either ignorant of what the Catholic Church teaches on birth control, or simply delinquent in their duty to tell young couples the truth. For my part, I had no idea I was doing anything that the Church taught was wrong. How was I to know, if the only people who could have told me, didn't? No one ever told me that IUDs were supposed to be painless, so when this one caused me discomfort I didn't think anything of it. Maybe it was the Lord's way of trying to penetrate my ignorance, to let me know something was amiss. If so, I missed the hint.

The day finally came when Paul was able to walk again without assistance. He told me he wanted to return to K-Mart and resume his career there, if he could, though it would likely mean moving away from our home and our friends. I wasn't eager to pull up stakes and start over in a strange place, but we talked it over thoroughly and I finally told Paul that if going back to K-Mart was what he thought was right, then I was with him.

K-Mart welcomed him back with open arms (as I knew they would) and promptly offered him an attractive management position—in Atlanta, Georgia. What a shock! Here we were with two little children, a terrific job offer, and no money.

We borrowed from every relative who had a dollar to spare, bought a used 1957 Dodge that gave new meaning to the word "klunker," piled our two little babies and our large German Shepherd dog into the back, and hit the road. We decided to go by way of Los Angeles, so that my parents could see the babies and so that my master-mechanic stepfather could fix up the car that was going to have to carry us to what, as far we were concerned, might as well have been the other side of the earth.

Our two weeks in Los Angeles were marvelous. My parents were delighted to spend so much time with their grandchildren, even though my mother's arthritis had advanced to the point where she had great difficulty even holding a baby for any length of time. I had the sinking feeling that she would soon be completely unable to move. But we did all we could to make our visit special for her.

From Los Angeles we set off on our trek. We crossed the southern tier of the country, finally arriving in Savannah, Georgia, on the Atlantic coast. Paul's mother and oldest brother lived there, and the kids and I bunked with them while Paul went on to Atlanta to find a place for us to live. Three weeks later we moved into a small, dirty, run-down rental house, got our furniture and belongings out of storage, and settled in to our new life. It wasn't much, but it was home. The stressfulness of the whole experience was reflected in my body in a very visible way. I had lost eighty pounds during the latter part of our Washington days. Now I gained them back.

Because we needed additional income, I took care of people's children during the day—and sometimes for a couple weeks at a time when their parents had to travel out of town on business. I was also able to volunteer some of my time on behalf of the local chapter of Birthright, which worked to provide housing for women who were pregnant and who might otherwise seek an abortion. I was able to collect items for Birthright baby showers while keeping the children in the car.

I soon came in contact with the leaders of Georgia Right to Life, a fledgling group just gearing up in early 1973. I assembled newsletters, stuffed them in envelopes, and dropped them off at the post office. The mailing list had only 200 names on it, but in those early days that seemed like a huge number.

Gradually things began to turn around for the Brown family. Paul's salary from K-Mart enabled us to get out of debt once and for all. It also enabled me to stop baby-sitting—a real blessing, as our own children needed more of my time. I lost the eighty pounds again.

I also increased my involvement with Birthright and with Georgia Right to Life. The Supreme Court had recently issued its infamous Roe v. Wade decision, which with a single stroke threw out the abortion laws of all fifty states, and for all practical purposes guaranteed abortion-on-demand at any point in the baby's prenatal development. Working for the pro-life cause now seemed to Paul and me to be a moral imperative.

Me, Paul, Cathy at five months, and two-and-a-half-year-old Hugh.

Though Paul was working seventy to eighty hours a week, he always made time to keep abreast of what was happening in the movement. There was a lot of optimism in those days that the Supreme Court's reckless action would swiftly be overturned by an act of Congress. Paul thought that optimism was naive, and foresaw a national tragedy of enormous proportions if abortion was indeed allowed to remain legal. I'm sad to say he turned out to be absolutely correct.

Before long Paul was promoted again, this time to a senior management position. As always, a promotion meant a relocation. This time we were off to Kannapolis, North Carolina, where, among other things, we finally learned what the Catholic Church really had to say about birth control.

I know it is difficult to understand how we remained ignorant of this teaching for so long. The truth, I suppose, is that we didn't really want to know the truth. We had been raised Catholic, and we understood the basics of the creed and the sacraments. We were going to Mass every Sunday and raising our children as good Catholics. In the early years of our marriage, when we sought out our pastor and a Catholic physician for advice on the subject of birth control, I suppose they simply told us what they thought we wanted to hear: that taking The Pill, or using an IUD, was acceptable. Second best, perhaps, but still "okay."

Our lack of understanding isn't all that surprising, I suppose; I still run into many people who, despite being lifelong Catholics, don't understand anything more about the Church's teaching in this area than we did.

But when our pastor in Kannapolis finally shared with us the Church's full teaching about the sanctity of marriage, the full meaning of the procreative act, and the evil of birth control as a denial of trust in God, we didn't hesitate. The IUD came out, once and for all.

Thus our move to Kannapolis signalled the start of a new era in an important part of our lives. As we were soon to learn, it signalled many other changes as well.

In the School
of Adversity

1973 - 1974

Dismiss all anxiety from your minds. Present your needs to God in every form of prayer and in petitions full of gratitude. Then God's own peace, which is beyond all understanding, will stand guard over your hearts and minds, in Christ Jesus.

Philippians 4:6-7

Chapter Seven

TALK ABOUT SENDING A LAMB into the lion's den! We had barely unpacked the moving crates when I suddenly found myself engaged in a public debate with Kannapolis' leading proponent of abortion.

It started innocently enough. We had been getting acquainted with our parish priest, who was trying to raise the parish's awareness of abortion, and who had decided that a public debate with the local abortionist would be a good idea. When he heard of my past involvement with Birthright and Georgia Right to Life, he decided I would be the perfect person to represent the pro-life side. And for some reason I'll never understand, I agreed to do it.

Remember, I had no training in debate, and no experience at it either; all I'd ever done as a pro-life volunteer was to stuff envelopes and transport items to garage sales. My opponent, Dr. Crosby (not his real name), was one of the most highly respected obstetrician/gynecologists in the area. He obviously wasn't too intimidated at the prospect of debating a pregnant (by this time our third little one was on the way) housewife from the rental district of Kannapolis. What would someone like me know about the complex issues surrounding abortion?

Good question. The answer was that I knew hardly anything about the complex issues. So I stuck to the simple ones: when my turn came to speak, I simply described what actually happens to a baby during an abortion procedure. This so unnerved Dr. Crosby that he literally got up and walked out of the room!

Lesson number one in Kannapolis: God uses those who are willing to be used, and he gives them whatever they need to accomplish the task he sets before them.

Life continued to be chaotic, even beyond the usual dislocations caused by moving. I had to go to work again, in order for us to send Hugh, who was now five, to a Christian kindergarten. I eventually found a job managing heating oil accounts for a local company. It only took me a few hours a day, which left me plenty of time to be home with Cathy.

Then we got the call that my mother was gravely ill. Somehow Paul scraped up enough money for me to fly home to California to see her. She was in the hospital with severe arthritis and bleeding ulcers, and at first I really thought it would be our last visit.

Mama eventually pulled through, but it required eight months in the hospital and the loss of most of her stomach. By the time she came home, she had lost her ability to walk.

This was a real blow to someone who had always done everything for everybody else. For a time she was extremely bitter. But Daddy was always there for her, loving her as much as ever, always patient, always kind.

Indeed, I have always looked back on my stepfather's conduct during this time as a prime example of Christ-like love, being willing to take up the cross, with all its pain, for the sake of the joy that lies on the other side of self-sacrifice. My stepfather never formally professed any religion. But I think he lived the gospel message better than many of us, who claim to know the way to salvation for ourselves and others!

That was lesson number two during this trying period: God loves a cheerful giver, and he blesses those who face hardship with faith, patience, and dignity.

Finally, life appeared to be settling down. I was back from California and, as my pregnancy entered the third trimester, I left my job with the heating oil company in order to prepare for the arrival of Baby Brown number three.

And what an arrival it was!

It was the middle of the night when my water broke, which is ordinarily a sign that the onset of labor isn't far off. Remembering how quickly Cathy had been delivered, we rushed right into the hospital for what we were sure would be a speedy labor and delivery. This was on the 17th of June.

But the 18th came, the labor escalated and then dropped off, and no baby. The 19th came. Again the labor escalated. Again it dropped. Again, no baby. All this time I was in a labor room with a bunch of wires taped to my tummy, monitoring the baby's heartbeat. After three days of false starts, that heartbeat had begun to grow quite weak. The doctors—and Paul and I, as well—were starting to get worried.

It soon became clear that the baby was in distress and that immediate steps had to be taken. Fortunately, Paul and I were told, the most accomplished doctor in the area happened to be on duty that night. He would be the best person imaginable to handle the situation. We couldn't be in better hands. You guessed it: it was my old debate foe, Dr. Crosby.

At that point, I really wasn't thinking about the debate, and Dr. Crosby was far too professional to let our past encounter color his attitudes. He sized up the situation and ordered an immediate Caesarian section. I wasn't too excited about the prospect of major surgery, but after three days of labor I just wanted to get that baby born! And so, within a few minutes, I was drifting off to the happy land of anesthesia.

What I didn't realize then was just how serious the situation really was. Unbeknownst to me, Paul and Dr. Crosby were discussing the likelihood that the baby would be stillborn. Not only that: given my history of difficult childbirths, and the prolonged labor I had already endured this time around, Dr. Crosby was concerned that I might not survive, either. I can only imagine the agonies that Paul must have suffered, pacing outside that operating room, awaiting the outcome of the operation.

As it turned out, he needn't have worried. The most skilled surgeon in the state delivered Christina Lee Brown at 9:37 p.m. on the evening of June 19. We had intended to name her Nancy, but in view of all that had happened, we thought Christina was a better reflection of our gratitude to the Lord. We named her Lee in honor of the woman who had suggested, several years before, that I make the acquaintance of a Mr. Paul Brown.

Christy's birth came almost three full days since my water

had broken. She was beautiful (of course!) and perfectly healthy. The only ill effect I suffered was an infection, which prevented me from holding her for five days. That was difficult, of course. But once I learned how grave the situation had been, waiting a few days to hold my baby didn't seem like such a hardship after all.

I had a fairly long recovery from Christy's birth. I spent part of my time writing to each of the hospital staff who had been so helpful to us during our long ordeal. I even wrote a letter to the editor of the local newspaper, praising Dr. Crosby's expertise. When I went in for my six-week checkup, I took Christy with me and asked Dr. Crosby if he would like to come out and see her. He looked at me in a very strange way and said, simply, "No. I can't."

I puzzled over his response for a long time. In retrospect, I suppose he must have been struggling with the conflict between his obvious talent for saving life and his conviction that it was all right to take life at the whim of the mother. Did it occur to him—as it certainly did to me—that had I been on another floor of the hospital that night, he would have been

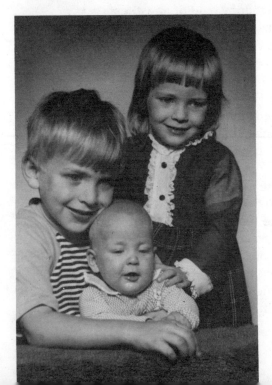

Hugh at five years, Cathy at three and Christy at four months.

killing Christy rather than saving her?

I don't know. I never had another opportunity to talk to him. I do know that at last report Dr. Crosby was no longer doing abortions himself, but was devoting much of his time to specializing in women with troublesome pregnancies. I'd like to think that his experience with Christy and me had something to do with that. I still pray for him, as I do for all present and former abortionists, that their hearts may be softened.

Lesson number three: God can use times of trial to touch the hardest of hearts. Thus it was, I believe, that he used Christy and me to help Dr. Crosby move a few steps forward in his awareness of the sanctity of life.

When Christy was eight months old, Paul was transferred to Steubenville, Ohio—his first job as manager of his own store. This kind of transfer typically took effect immediately, which meant that the family—in this case, us—was left behind, sometimes for several weeks. Paul flew to Steubenville one Monday morning to get acquainted with his staff, take over operations at the store, and start looking for a home for us.

The very next day Christy developed a fever—a very high fever. Her temperature went up to 105 degrees. I called the pediatrician, who suggested I give her an alcohol bath. Her temperature went down for a while, but spiked again a few hours later. I gave her another alcohol bath, and her temperature went down as it had before. Unfortunately, it also went back up again. By three in the morning she was in convulsions, and I was nearly in a panic. I frantically called neighbors until I was able to borrow a car and get the other kids watched. Then I raced off to the hospital, praying all the while that Christy would be all right.

When we arrived, the emergency room staff took Christy from me, rushed her into an examining room with the doors slamming shut behind them, and didn't communicate with me again for several hours. When the doctor finally came out, his expression was grim. Christy was now in a coma. They had given her a spinal tap, fearing that she might have spinal meningitis. She might or might not survive.

Little Christy lay in her crib in the intensive-care unit for two days, with an IV in her head, without moving. I was beside myself. The worst part was that I had been unable to communicate with Paul through all this. Since we were in the process of moving, our home phone had been disconnected; I had to rely on the assistant manager of the local K-Mart store to convey messages to Paul at the Steubenville store. Though I sent several urgent messages, for some reason no one even tried to contact him until the third day, when Christy finally came out of the coma.

It happened just that suddenly, too: three days after I had rushed her to the hospital, she woke up, her fever returned to normal, and she broke out in a bright red rash from head to toe. Her problem was not spinal meningitis, but a case of roseola measles.

Lesson number four: In our weakest moments, in the midst of our most terrible fears, when we feel most alone—even then our Lord is at our side, working his will in our lives. Without Paul there to lead me, I had to handle Christy's crisis all alone. I learned, for the first time, that I did indeed have the strength to cope with such an ordeal.

By the time Paul finally got word of Christy's condition, she was already out of danger. By the time he got back to Kannapolis to be with us, I was more than ready to leave! We had weathered a great many trials there, and even though I can see how the Lord used each experience to prepare us for what lay ahead, it was still extremely difficult at the time.

There were so many tests in such a short period of time that I occasionally doubted my ability to cope. I can remember times of crying, then laughing, then crying again, wanting nothing more than to hang onto my dear husband and never let him go again. Even though we had survived it all, I never wanted to go through it again. I just wanted to tell Paul how much I loved him, and how much I hoped we would never be separated again.

Hello, Congressman!

1975 - 1976

Chapter Eight

SETTLING INTO OUR NEW life in Steubenville was a real challenge.

All three children became ill almost immediately upon our arrival in town, and we had no idea what was causing it. We had more coughs, more colds, and more ear infections than I ever imagined three human beings could have in the course of twelve months—which turned out to be the total length of our stay in Steubenville.

Soon after we moved into our townhome, we set about the usual scavenger hunt, which I'm sure is familiar to anyone who has ever had to relocate because of a career: we searched out a good pediatrician, located our parish and got to know the pastor, Fr. Robert Mascolino. Hugh, who was to enter first grade, got his first Catholic school uniform, and caught the bus every morning right in front of our home. Cathy and Christy shared a bedroom and got along about as well as two sisters ever do when they share a bedroom.

We had been attending our new parish for about three months when a notice appeared in the bulletin announcing a pro-life meeting. Upper Ohio Valley Right to Life was looking for new members. This was 1975, and even though the Roe v. Wade decision had been in force for more than two years, awareness of the reality of child-killing still had not sifted down to grass-roots America, even among Christians.

At the meeting, the leaders mentioned that they needed an editor for the newsletter. I volunteered. They also mentioned the need to identify a local business that would let them sell pro-life Christmas cards on the sidewalk. Paul offered the Kresge store that he now managed. The card sale was a great success, and opened the way to bake sales, a flea market, and many other activities that raised much-needed funds for our group and helped us spread the word about the plight of the preborn.

I was soon chosen to represent our chapter at meetings of the Ohio Right to Life Society, which is where I met the man who really taught me how to be an articulate pro-life spokesman. I am referring, of course, to our state chairman, Dr. John C. Willke. He spoke with eloquence and ease, he emphasized the sanctity of all life and the child's right to life from the moment of conception, and he underlined the importance of faith in doing pro-life work.

In January, 1976, Upper Ohio Valley Right to Life asked me to go to the March for Life, in Washington, D.C.—it would be held on the third anniversary of Roe—and to represent them at a special breakfast with members of Congress.

I was thrilled, of course. I even made myself a new suit for the occasion. I had to: thanks to the stresses of the last couple years in Kannapolis and now in Steubenville, I had regained most of my excess weight. Our finances were also such that I

Below: Cathy, age eight months.

Right: Hugh teasing Cathy.

had to make most of the clothes for myself and the children. I loved every minute of the sewing, especially for our dainty daughters, and was glad to be able to afford something new when a special occasion arose.

And the trip to Washington was definitely a special occasion. The day before the march, I went to a meeting sponsored by the March for Life Corporation. The president, Nellie Gray, spoke brilliantly for forty minutes about standing for our principles, about God's blessing of new life, and about our call to be soldiers in the war against innocent, preborn children. That speech made such an impact on me that to this day, whenever I think of it, the same feelings of excitement and resolve well up within me. I wanted to do more for the preborn. I wanted to be closer to the action. That night I prayed that our Lord would somehow make it happen. It was a fateful prayer, as I was soon to learn!

The next day I had breakfast with our Congressman, Wayne Hayes. He was getting a lot of unfavorable publicity at the time, because of his cavortings with his attractive "secretary," Elizabeth Ray. Though I was less than impressed with his commitment to family values, I had learned from my experience with Dr. Crosby that God never gives up on anyone, and I talked my head off that morning about the babies, and the need to protect them. He listened politely, then gave his political justification for doing nothing. It was a speech I was to hear many times, in many forms, from many politicians down through the years.

Frustrated by my encounter with Congressman Hayes, but still invigorated by the March for Life and especially by Nellie Gray, I arrived back in Steubenville on fire for the pro-life cause. I told Paul I had prayed that he would be transferred to the Washington area. His response was immediate and emphatic: "That is the last !@#^$@ place on earth I'd ever want to live!"

Well, two weeks later Paul was transferred. Care to guess where?

Paul fussed and stewed about it, but eventually he accepted the transfer. It was a promotion, which meant more prestige within the company, more money, and better benefits. I called Dr. Willke and told him of our impending move. He promised to introduce me to Dr. Mildred Jefferson, president of the National Right to Life Committee, so that I could volunteer my time there if I wished. I then went to the Upper Ohio Valley chapter to relinquish my various responsibilities. By this time we had managed to build up an active membership, so the transfer wasn't difficult.

It had been an eventful year in Steubenville—a year that launched Paul and me into pro-life work once and for all. We had learned a lot. Still, I was glad to leave. We had eventually isolated the cause of the kids' health problems in the coal dust that settled over the city every morning, but though I learned some cleaning and air-filtration techniques that made things a bit better, they still suffered. Now we stood on the brink of what we sensed would be a grand adventure. I paused then, as I do now, to pay tribute to some wonderful people who cared, who sacrificed, who persisted in their efforts on behalf of the babies.

To Pauline Hoagland, whose involvement was without guile, I express gratitude for her patient, tender concern for each and every one of us who worked with her. To Guy Traversa, who is now with the Lord, I pay tribute to his efforts to lead the local Knights of Columbus to the forefront of the pro-life effort with spiritual, financial, and physical support. I express my admiration to Susan Krantz, who struggled to speak out even as she placed the needs of her own children first. And to all the others, I simply say thank you for being there when it was anything but popular to be pro-life in Steubenville, Ohio.

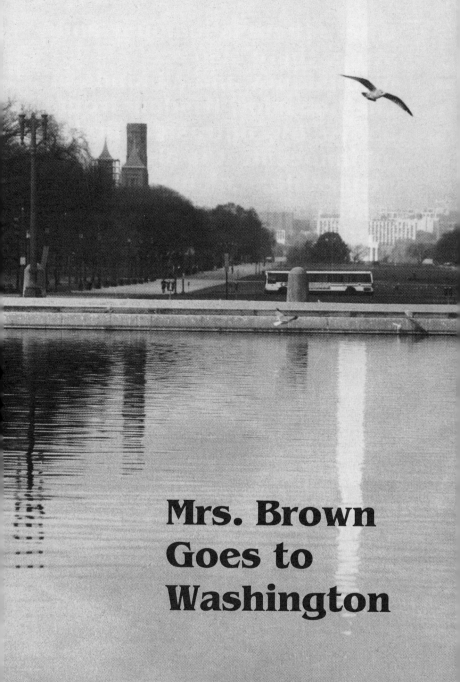

Mrs. Brown
Goes to
Washington

1976 - 1979

Where there is jealousy and strife, there also are inconstancy and all kinds of vile behavior. Wisdom from above, by contrast, is first of all innocent. It is also peaceable, lenient, docile, rich in sympathy and the kindly deeds that are its fruits, impartial and sincere. The harvest of justice is sown in peace for those who cultivate peace.

James 3:16-18

Chapter Nine

WE MOVED TO WASHINGTON with the usual Brown family flair: Cathy, Christy, Hugh, and Mom (that's me) all had the chicken pox. If you are an adult who has never had the chicken pox, I don't recommend it. I really got sick. Poor Paul had to take care of everyone all by himself, right in the midst of getting settled in a new home and a new job.

In time, life got back to normal (whatever "normal" is for a crew like ours!). Paul had found a townhome for us in Woodbridge, Virginia, about thirty miles south of Washington. Hugh and Cathy started school—Cathy was in kindergarten now—and Christy stayed home with me.

But I myself didn't stay home for long. In April of 1976 I ventured into the city to visit the offices of National Right to Life, to meet with Dr. Mildred Jefferson and the rest of the staff. "The rest of the staff" turned out to be only two other people. It seemed that the executive director had left several months before and had not yet been replaced; activity was at an all-time low; even the remaining two women had little to do because the phones seldom rang and almost no mail came in.

Dr. Jefferson still had a dynamic vision of NRLC as an umbrella organization under which all the other pro-life efforts in the country could come together. And she still had a tremendous flair with the media. What she needed was someone with business experience, someone who could shape things up and get things moving and put a spark into the operation—someone like me! Before I knew it I had signed on.

On the one hand, it was a dream come true. I would be able to do the thing that meant more to me than anything else in the world: help save the babies. And I would be able to do it alongside Dr. Jefferson, which would be a pleasure and an honor like no other.

On the other hand . . . I still had three small children, ages eight, six, and three. Until now I had considered myself a full-time, stay-at-home mom; working full time outside the house was not what I had bargained for. But the opportunity proved too tempting to resist. I put all three kids in a private school.

It was, to say the least, stressful. I was able to carpool into the city with Paul and two others, but it meant leaving the house at 6 a.m. Believe it or not, by leaving at that ungodly hour, we were just able to arrive at our destinations by 8 a.m. We got back home at 6 p.m., after stopping to pick up the kids.

I maintained this pace for two years. During that time, we did manage to significantly enhance the effectiveness of NRLC. We expanded to twenty employees, six times the office space, and immeasurably greater national prominence. I was consumed with it; I worked at home on nights and weekends, giving over every waking hour that wasn't directly taken up with immediate family necessities. Still, looking back, I have to say it wasn't worth the price I paid by putting my vocation to the pro-life cause—important as it was—ahead of my vocation as a wife and mother.

Finally I had to scale back. The immediate reason was that we bought a new house ten miles farther away from the city. The logistics of travel and child care, which had always been ridiculously complicated, now became simply impossible. And besides, it was time to make my own life correspond to my pro-family convictions by becoming a real wife and mother again.

I met with Dr. Jefferson and told her I was putting my kids (now ten, eight, and five) in a normal parish school, and that I would be leaving the office at two o'clock every afternoon so I could be there when they got home. I was going to clean the house and do the laundry and cook dinner again. She consented without hesitation. I felt a great sense of relief.

It didn't last long. Things were changing for Paul, just as they had for me.

Essentially, Paul was feeling that he had outgrown the opportunities available to him with K-Mart, and he wanted to get away from the pressure, the 80-hour work weeks, and the constant specter of having to pull up stakes and relocate every year or two. Like me, he longed for a more normal home life. And, like me, he wanted to do more for the babies.

A few months before, Paul had helped found something called the Life Amendment Political Action Committee, or LAPAC. Its goal was to mobilize money, manpower, and political clout against pro-abortion political candidates, and to support those who were pro-life.

The idea had come from the noble, but doomed, presidential campaign of Ellen McCormack in 1976. Paul, who was a great student of politics and a fanatic about the need for effective political action on behalf of the pro-life cause, greatly admired Mrs. McCormack and her band of dedicated supporters. They had shown how far a determined candidate could go, carrying the message of the sanctity of life and the need to defend each and every unborn child, bucking the political system, getting by on a shoestring budget. Surely, Paul thought, a national political action committee could do the same kind of thing across the country, by doing nothing more than making public where the various candidates stood on abortion.

LAPAC did indeed start on a shoestring. Its founders—Paul, Dr. Robert L. Sassone, and Morton Downey, Jr. (yes, the infamous television talk-show host)—were passionately committed to making a difference for the babies, but all had full-time jobs. They and their small group of volunteers were extremely limited in what they could accomplish.

But all that changed one Sunday evening when Paul went to Mass. The kids were sick and we were going to Mass on "split shifts," so Paul was by himself. When he came home, he simply announced that he was resigning his job the next morning. Without a moment's hesitation I replied, "Great!"

He later told me it was the sermon that had moved him to take such a bold step. The theme had been, "The only things of value in this life are the things you can take with you into eternity." He realized, he said, that he didn't want to retire from a company where his main achievement was keeping his toothpaste displays in order. Being a store manager, despite its prestige and good pay, was not fulfilling his desire to make his mark on the world, so that his children might have a better and more loving place to raise their families. And besides, he pointed out, America was killing one-and-a-half-million babies a year. It had to stop.

So Paul took a gamble and decided to put all his time and energy into developing LAPAC. Fundraising was the first priority, of course; in addition to backing pro-life candidates and giving the pro-life movement the political credibility it so desperately needed, he had a family to feed! But with the moral support of NRLC's board of directors—they had no political action committee of their own, and were glad to see one forming—and the aide of some expert advisors, LAPAC quickly got on the move.

Its impact was felt as early as the 1978 election campaign, when LAPAC helped defeat several notable pro-abortion senators, such as Birch Bayh of Indiana, George McGovern of South Dakota, and others. Paul appeared on numerous national television programs, and NBC even ran a segment about LAPAC during "Weekend," its popular news and features program. People magazine ran a four-page feature on Paul and Judie Brown and their three children. All in all, it was a dramatic step

People magazine featured me and American Life League in their January 22, 1979, issue.

forward for the pro-life movement. Finally we would be taken seriously in the political arena for our ability to help elect—and defeat—candidates for office.

My own world began to collapse just as Paul's was coming together. Trouble was brewing at NRLC. Some of the leadership wanted to co-opt LAPAC, bringing it under NRLC control. Paul would have none of it; he and the other board members felt that independence was a key to LAPAC's effectiveness. That led to some strained relationships at NRLC.

At the same time, I became more aware of various internal struggles at NRLC. When Dr. Jefferson left in June, 1978, I realized the degree to which she had been protecting me from NRLC's office politics. It was the usual sort of infighting and power struggles that occur in any organization, let alone one made up of more than fifty zealous, energetic human beings. But it discouraged me just the same. Paul urged me to stay on and try to make a difference. But by early 1979, it was clear to me that I simply had to leave.

In addition to the various other hassles, I found myself increasingly unable to support NRLC's views on a number of key issues. As far as I was concerned, there was no such thing as compromise when you were trying to save babies. That was the lesson I had learned from people such as Nellie Gray, Mildred Jefferson, Fr. Paul Marx, Dr. Murray Norris, Dr. Charles Rice, and other prominent national pro-life spokesmen. But NRLC was dismayingly silent on such subjects as abortifacient birth control devices, and it endorsed a political strategy that left the door open to abortion in certain cases.

As far as I was—and am—concerned, the baby in the womb

NRLC Convention, Chicago, June 18, 1977.

is a human being, entitled to the full rights of a human being, whether that baby has been in the womb one day or six months, and whether the result of marital union or a result of rape or incest. That is the starting point, the fundamental reality, that must underlie all our efforts.

Thus, when we know that some birth control devices, such as the IUD, actually work by inducing early abortions, we must oppose them, period. And when we know that each and every child in the womb is a human being (not to mention an American citizen, fully protected by the Constitution), we dare not suggest that some babies may not be worth saving—may legitimately be candidates for death—because of the circumstances of their conception. Rape and incest are unspeakably evil acts. But the baby in the womb is an innocent child, not the perpetrator. He or she deserves to be protected, not punished—especially when the punishment is a cruel and painful death.

We must be unflinchingly consistent in our philosophy, or we lose all credibility and moral force. Yes, the politician may have to settle for half-measures at times, out of political expediency. But you and I, who stand for nothing if not for the complete and final eradication of abortion, can never let ourselves be perceived as supportive of anything that denies the personhood of any unborn child. Personhood is our absolute. We cannot waver from it.

So, in March, 1979, I resigned from NRLC.

I want to make clear that I have never viewed any individual at NRLC as being anything less than totally committed to the proposition that each and every abortion is murder and must be stopped. But I was unhappy with NRLC's strategy in pursuing its aims. I was afraid their approach would make it too easy for politicians to get away with statements such as "I am personally opposed to abortion, but . . ." and "I am against abortion, except . . ." To my way of thinking, then and now, there can be no "buts" and no "excepts" when it comes to saving the babies. If we retreat from our absolutes—if we start settling, philosophically, for incremental change—then our effectiveness is ended and our movement is dead.

A Telegram
From Heaven

1979 - 1981

Trust in the
Lord with all
your heart,
on your own
intelligence
rely not;

In all your ways
be mindful of
him, he will
make straight
your paths.

Proverbs 3:5-6

Chapter Ten

I T WAS ON MARCH 1, 1979, that I dropped my letter of resignation in the mail to NRLC. The sound of that letter hitting the bottom of the mailbox seemed to trigger the most extraordinary sequence of events I had ever experienced. It was as if the Lord had been waiting to communicate with me about what he wanted me to do next, and my leaving NRLC made that communication possible. And what a communication it was! I have always referred to the entire experience as "receiving a telegram from heaven."

Paul and I had been invited to a reception in Washington that afternoon. After mailing my resignation letter, I phoned Paul to tell him what I had just done, and to tell him I was on my way to meet him. While I was driving downtown, Paul got another phone call. It was from Morton Blackwell, an associate of the conservative direct-mail fundraising guru, Richard Viguerie. He said that Mr. Viguerie was interested in providing start-up funds for a new pro-life group and was looking for someone to head up the effort. I was Mr. Viguerie's first choice, Morton said, but they knew I was loyally committed to NRLC, and wondered if we might be able to recommend someone else.

Paul just laughed. "Morton," he said, "you're not going to believe this, but . . ."

That is how the odyssey of American Life Lobby and American Life League began.

Within a month I had met with Mr. Viguerie to discuss ideas, engaged an attorney to help with the paperwork, and met several times with our pro-life friends Robert L. Sassone and Gabrielle Avery (who has since gone to be with the Lord). Sitting around the dining room table in our home, we selected a name for our new organization, invited Gabrielle's husband, Walter, to serve as its first treasurer, and directed our lawyer to start drawing up papers for two non-profit corporations: one oriented to influencing lawmakers (American Life Lobby), the other oriented to educating the public about pro-life issues (American Life League).

It took a few months to work out all the details. I stayed home during that time, helping Paul with LAPAC, caring for the children, and developing ideas for ALL About Issues, our organization's newsletter, which I wrote on my IBM Selectric typewriter and distributed using LAPAC's copier and addressograph machine.

I also wound up spending a fair amount of time working through some personal struggles. My last months at NRLC, and my eventual decision to leave, had been very hard on me. Some of the time I felt anger. Some of the time I felt self-pity. Almost all of the time I felt confusion. I never questioned whether I had done the right thing, but I had to deal with a lot of emotional turmoil. Finally I decided that there was simply

Me working at home on *ALL About Issues,* the organization newsletter in its infancy.

Me reviewing *ALL About Issues* with 1980 Editor, Edwin Elliot, Jr.

nothing I could do about what had happened—but with God's grace, there was a great deal I could do to help other pro-life people become better soldiers for the Lord in the battle to stop the slaughter of the innocents.

By October, we were ready for our first fundraising effort. We had no mailing list of our own at all, and so we had to start from scratch. The Viguerie company would rent lists of names of people they thought might be pro-life, and then simply send letters to them, describing our new organization and asking them to support it. It was slow going for a while. In those days, being the director of A.L.L. meant that I was the one who counted the money, wrote the thank-you letters, and answered the phone calls. I was the only "staff" we had!

I must say our children were quite pleased with this whole turn of events, because they got to have Mom at home all the time. I liked it, too: I knew the kids were at an age when it was important for me to be there for them, and now I was able to do that. The kids grew in their pro-life convictions, too. Even Christy, at the tender age of five, knew that abortion killed babies and was quick to say so to anyone who looked like he needed to be told.

By the following spring—March, 1980—American Life Lobby had grown to a point where it could hire two part-time staffers. This was when I really began to appreciate our community of Stafford, Virginia. We found people who were capable, committed, and more interested in saving babies than in making money (which was fortunate, since we couldn't afford to pay much!). The circulation of ALL About Issues was growing, and we decided to publish it in a newspaper format and put it out once a month. It had always been my philosophy—and still is—that the best thing I could do to help save the babies was to arm others with the ammunition they needed to be effective in the field. Even in those early days, ALL About Issues was a valuable asset to thousands of people who were working to save the babies.

My own thinking about pro-life work went through an important change at this time as well. I had once again regained those troublesome eighty pounds, partly from the stress of starting up a new organization, and partly because I had not yet learned the importance of consistent dependence on the Lord.

To be sure, I believed that God was guiding our family, and me, and A.L.L. I often thought back on the extraordinary events of March, 1979, when my time with NRLC ended and my time with A.L.L. started, all on the same afternoon. It was as though the Lord simply picked me up from the ashes, without the least bit of planning on my part. All I'd known was that I had to be a better wife and mother, and I had to leave NRLC. I'd had no thought of leading a group, speaking in public (let alone on television!), or any of the other astonishing things that were about to come my way.

I did know that no single person, no single group, and no single political party was going to stop the killing. God, and God alone, would end this horrible crime if and when the people of our nation sought him and his will for them, rather than their own convenience.

I was finally beginning to learn that we not only can but must trust in the Lord rather than in our own pitifully weak resources. You and I cannot change minds, soften hardened hearts, or prick the conscience of a nation—but our Lord can do all these things, and will do them if we but trust in him. I was beginning to learn that I really wasn't such a smart cookie after all—but that the Lord was willing to use me anyway.

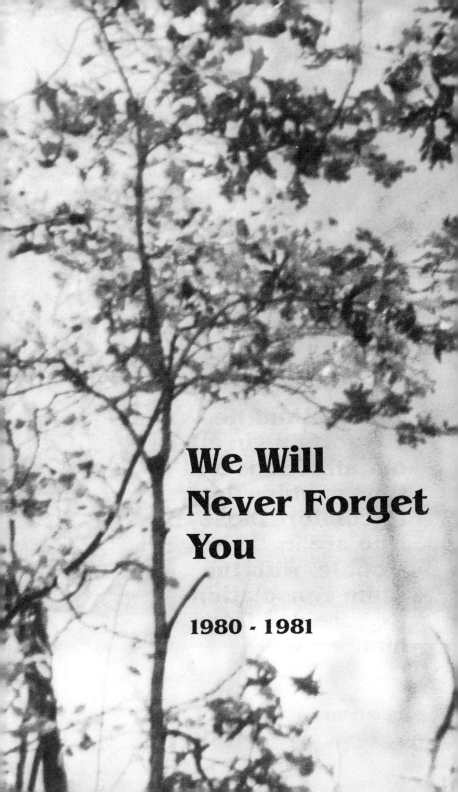

**We Will
Never Forget
You**

1980 - 1981

Praised be God,
the Father of our
Lord Jesus Christ,
the Father of
mercies, and the
God of all
consolation! He
comforts us in all
our afflictions and
thus enables us
to comfort those
who are in
trouble, with the
same consolation
we received from
him.

2 Corinthians 1:3-4

Chapter Eleven

WE ALL KNEW THAT MY mother's condition was steadily deteriorating. I spoke with her by phone as often as I could, as well as with my father, who told me of her diminishing ability to do even such simple things as pick up a cup of coffee.

We had already had one crisis with Mama, in 1976, at the height of the chaotic time when I was working twelve-hour days at NRLC. I'd had to make two emergency trips to Southern California to be with her. She had pulled through, however, and had even been able to spend Christmas with us that year—as it turned out, the last trip she was ever to take.

Now, in the summer of 1980, Paul and I loaded up the children and made the trek to Los Angeles, wondering whether it would be our last visit with Mama. To our relief, the visit went extraordinarily well. Though Mama couldn't move without assistance, she was a joy to be with. I was glad to see her able to enjoy her grandchildren—and vice versa.

We had been back home only a few weeks when, in the fall, Daddy had a heart attack. Back to California I went. The doctors wanted to perform quadruple-bypass surgery, to which we all agreed. My sisters and I split the time caring for Mama, and then for Daddy as well when he left the hospital. It soon became clear that Daddy was going to be fine—indeed, he would likely be in better health than he had in years—but that Mama's suffering was only going to get worse, and her situation more serious. I went back home with a heavy heart.

I decided to set active pro-life work on the shelf for several weeks, so that I could devote the holidays to family concerns. Paul and I decided I should go back to California for Thanksgiving. We ourselves had much to be thankful for: our own family was stable, A.L.L. was off to a good start, and Paul had founded a management consulting firm in addition to LAPAC, which was also flourishing. The temporary absence of one housewife from the pro-life scene was obviously not going to make a decisive difference. The opportunity to be with my parents again—to cook the Thanksgiving turkey—was a blessing beyond measure.

Unfortunately, the impact on me of the various stresses of family and career was measurable, particularly around my waist. I seemed to find solace only in food. I ate Christmas candy by the pound, as well as anything else I happened to prepare, serve, or come within reach of. By the end of the year I had gained an additional twenty pounds. Paul's mother, who stayed with us at Christmas, expressed concern over my weight, but I tuned her out. After all, she didn't understand the problems I was dealing with.

In early 1981 I made my first appearance on television. The

My mother was bedridden by 1980, but loved being with her grandchildren. *Back left to right:* Mama, Joanna, Kimberly, Christy. *Front left to right:* Cathy, Dana, and Hugh.

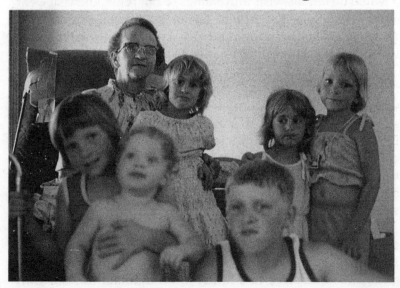

show was called "A.M. Washington," hosted by Carol Randolph. I was to debate a woman from the National Abortion Rights Action League. I arrived early, wearing my best black-and-white print dress. Needless to say, I was excited.

My excitement—that is to say, my nervousness—pretty much overwhelmed whatever effectiveness I might have had. But what happened during the program was far less memorable than what happened afterward. Carol took me aside and offered me some hints on how to dress for television. A woman of thirty-six who carried as much weight as I did should never, ever wear a print, she said, or a short dress, or a hairdo that was high and full around the face.

In retrospect I can only confirm how right she was. I went on the air that day wearing a dress that emphasized every single pound I carried, a hairdo straight out of the '60s, and no makeup at all. I have often joked that the pro-life cause was represented in that debate by the Bride of Bozo! It was, if nothing else, a lesson in humility. I took Carol Randolph's advice and never again wore a print in public. I did not, however, lose the excess weight.

Then one morning I received the phone call I had been dreading for so long. Daddy called to tell me that Mama was gravely ill and that I had better come at once if I wanted to see her alive one last time. Paul immediately called the airline, helped me pack, and drove me to the airport; my brother-in-law met me at the other end and took me straight to my parents' home. I dropped my luggage in a heap inside the front door and went immediately to my mother's bedside.

We talked for about fifteen minutes. I still remember her smile and the sparkle in her beautiful brown eyes as she told me she was ready to die. She only hoped that God would forgive her for the many times she had blamed him for her poor health.

At 4:30 the next morning, Daddy woke me up to tell me that Mama had just passed away.

The rest of the day was a blur, handling the countless details of arranging the funeral. I couldn't help but marvel at my stepfather. For ten years he had cared for Mama, and been at her side every minute he was not at work or asleep. He made sure he came home for lunch each day to check on her. No matter what was on his mind, no matter how tired he may have been, no matter how much he might rather have been taking a break, he was always there for Mama. He brought to life for me the words of St. Paul, that God comforts us in our afflictions in order that we might be able to comfort others. He has always been for me the embodiment of the compassion we are meant to show to one another.

I wept all the way home from Los Angeles. I had lost my closest friend in the world. But I also felt relieved, knowing that Mama was at peace, without pain, and in the presence of the God she loved so dearly.

I had barely recovered from the wrenching emotional ordeal of Mama's death when a new crisis hit. One Saturday morning, Christy—now seven years old—came running into the house to tell me that Cathy had fallen off her bike and was lying in the gravel. "She's dead, Mommy, she's dead!" Christy cried.

I rushed outside to find Cathy writhing on the ground, screaming in pain. By the time the ambulance had arrived, we had determined that the pain was in her leg. It turned out that

Cathy and I, bonding during her hospital stay with her leg in traction, in 1980.

she had broken her femur—the largest bone in her leg—at the hip. It was a very serious break indeed. Fortunately, one of the best orthopedic surgeons in the East was on call that day; he inserted a pin in her leg and placed her in traction. Cathy spent six weeks in the hospital wearing a full body cast, and I spent most of those six weeks at her side, trying to keep up with the mail and help Paul hold the fort at home.

By the time Cathy came out of the hospital on crutches, I had gained yet another 20 pounds and now tipped the scales at a whopping 250! I could wear only elastic-waisted pants, and even they bulged. I told people I bought all my outfits from "Omar the Tentmaker."

In the meantime, pro-life work was enveloping our household like a giant squid. A.L.L. now had six employees, all of whom worked in our previously unfinished basement, which Paul had had to finish just to provide some modest office space. By the end of 1980 we had more than 35,000 names on our mailing list, and the amount of work was growing just as

1981: American Life Lobby presents Senator Jesse Helms with the Hero of the Year Award. Left-to-right, Dick Walters, Me, Senator Helms, and Paul.

rapidly: mail to open, requests to answer, letters to write, resource materials to compile.

In March, 1981—the month Mama died—we added two more staff members. There was no more room in the basement, so we put them to work in the dining room upstairs. Paul decided that was the last straw. When things got to the point where the children felt like intruders in their own home, he said, it was time to send the pro-life movement packing! And that was just what we did: Paul bought an old, run-down building, which became A.L.L.'s new headquarters. In September we moved again, into a completely refurbished office building with space for a computer room, and proper offices for the staff. Pro-life groups that had once doubted our credibility were beginning to accept the new kid on the block.

That newly won clout quickly became important to us. In October, we began to tackle something called the Hatch Amendment. This proposed amendment to the Constitution, which was endorsed by some pro-life groups, would simply have said that the right to an abortion was not guaranteed and that all further considerations were up to the states to decide.

A.L.L. could not accept such an amendment, which ignored the absolute personhood of every unborn child and left open the possibility that abortion might be an acceptable option. If that was the best the pro-life movement could do, we felt, then we all might as well pack our bags and leave Washington. We argued, we debated, we testified, we prayed, we fasted, and in the end we defeated the Hatch Amendment.

The battle over the Hatch Amendment caused a deep division in the pro-life movement, leaving two distinct camps with two distinct ways of looking at the unborn baby. One camp said that "something was better than nothing" when it came to limiting abortion, and thus was willing to accept partial solutions. A.L.L. was—and is—totally unwilling to settle for anything less than a complete halt to the slaughter. Our view has never changed: that every life is precious and must be protected from the moment of conception.

True Vocation

1982 - 1983

Let hearts rejoice who search for the Lord. Seek the Lord and his strength, seek always the face of the Lord.

Psalm 104:3-4

Chapter Twelve

THE YEAR 1982 was a year of transition for our pro-life work and for me personally. It began with the annual get-together of pro-life leaders with the president on the anniversary of the Roe v. Wade decision. President Reagan really invigorated us with his strong expression of desire that abortion be stopped.

But the fact of the matter was that political action in the pro-life arena was weakening, diluted by the compromising attitudes of so many leaders and groups. It had reached the point where politicians could get away with adopting the "pro-life" label merely by opposing taxpayer funding of abortion, without expressing any commitment to the absolute personhood of the preborn child.

Paul decided the time had come to step down from his position with the Life Amendment Political Action Committee (LAPAC). This was due in part to his frustration over the state of affairs in the political-action realm, and in part to a desire to separate LAPAC from A.L.L. in people's minds. In reality, the only link between the two groups was the fact that their respective directors happened to be married to each other, but people understandably tended to assume they were all part of the same organization. So Paul handed over the reins of LAPAC to others, and focused his energies on his consulting business and on serving as my chief advisor at A.L.L.

Our work there was continuing to expand, both in size and influence. American Life League now had more than 75,000 supporters. ALL About Issues had become a forty-eight-page magazine circulated to more than 100,000 people in more than thirty countries. Though we had not yet stopped legalized abortion, I believe that we had helped save more babies by equipping people to work against abortion from the pulpit, in the classroom, and on the sidewalks in front of the abortion clinics.

Just as things were going so well, Ash Wednesday arrived—and with it a lawsuit. It had to do with a contractual dispute involving American Life Lobby and the company that was handling our direct mail fundraising. Frankly, we had grown so fast, and with so little experience at running a big organization, that we had trouble staying on top of the endless details involved in such a big operation. In time we were able to settle the lawsuit amicably, and in a way that made us stronger as an organization. But at the time, it was a real blow. It had the capacity to cripple American Life Lobby, and to threaten the effectiveness of American Life League, which was by far the larger of the two entities.

I did two things that Ash Wednesday in response to the lawsuit. First, I went to our lawyer. Second, I went to Mass. I felt

The Brown family, Christmas 1983.

as though this latest crisis was going to drive me over the edge unless something major happened. As it turned out, something major did happen. The Lord used the situation to bring me, at long last, fully to himself.

It didn't start out all that "spiritual." I prayed vigorously that the Lord would help us deal with the lawsuit, and in a way that would enable both the Lobby and the League to remain in operation. I told him that if he would help us out of the mess we were in, I would lose 100 pounds.

I know, I know: you're not supposed to make deals with God. But I didn't really think of it that way at the time. I simply had problems that were too big for me to handle, and I was asking the Lord to take charge of everything in my life— including my gluttony.

My prayers having been prayed, I set about reviewing every aspect of my life, beginning with my commitment to my vocation of being a wife and mother. I had been so moody and irritable with Paul and the kids, it was a wonder they hadn't strung me up long before. A number of things began to become clear to me.

First, as a "pro-life leader," I really thought I had all the answers and that victory would come about because of my efforts. Wrong!

I felt that my husband and children should accept the fact that pro-life work demanded most of my waking hours, including evenings and weekends, and that housekeeping, cooking, and laundry were not matters I needed to be concerned with. Wrong!

When I did prepare meals, I felt we shouldn't let anything go to waste, and that every morsel of food not consumed by someone else had to be consumed by me. Wrong!

I felt that being in church with God once a week should be enough for anyone. Wrong—at least for me.

One by one the scales fell from my eyes. It was suddenly clear that I had to make immense changes in my life if I was ever to realize my hopes and dreams—especially my desire to one day see my mother again in heaven. I felt that the words of the book of Revelation applied to me:

The Washington Times   FRIDAY, JANUARY 20, 1984 / PAGE 5C

Q&A

Pro-lifers are seeking wider support for their campaign

Paul and Judie Brown on the American Life Lobby Inc.

Paul and Judie Brown have long been in the vanguard of the pro-life movement. Mrs. Brown, president of the American Life Lobby Inc., has been called the "Joan of Arc" of the pro-life movement. Her husband is director of the Life Amendment Political Action Committee. They were interviewed by Washington Times columnist Tom Diaz.

Q: Sunday will mark the 11th anniversary of the Supreme Court's decision in Roe vs. Wade — the so-called right-to-abortion decision. Where does the movement stand on this anniversary?

Mr. Brown: We stand at a crossroads, a point at which we must make decisions as to new goals for the movement. We've had success in the political arena, the legislative arena. But until we conquer the intelligentsia of this country and are able to match and refute more of things that are put out by our opponents through vehicles like the Alan Guttmacher Institute, we'll have trouble succeeding, making bigger and better steps in the future. So, one of the goals we have for 1984 is to open a Human Life Institute.

Q: What is the Alan Guttmacher Institute?

Mr. Brown: It's a think tank of the pro-abortion movement. They do many, many studies, most of them government-financed. And, to date, they go unrefuted because there is no comparable vehicle for the pro-life movement.

Q: You say they're government-financed. There was a lot of talk three years ago when the new administration came in that this financing of ideological and political points of view was going to end. Is that still going on?

Mrs. Brown: Unfortunately, Planned Parenthood Federation of America, which is the parent organization of the Institute, has been defined by the Internal Revenue Service — long before the Reagan administration — as an education effort. Therefore, even though they lobby extensively on Capitol Hill with taxpayer dollars and repeatedly deny that they do so, it has been impossible for us to impact on the Reagan administration to remove their funding, even though we have tried repeatedly through various courses of action.

One of the reasons is that when we are asked by members of the administration to provide studies to prove our point of view, we have been unable to provide adequate studies. That's why we want to start this institute, so that we can compete study-for-study with our opponents when it comes to federal funding for future studies, with enough credibility to earn the same kind of multimillion-dollar grants that are presently going exclusively to our opposition.

Q: How would you assess the situation on Capitol Hill?

Mrs. Brown: Grim, as far as the pro-life movement is concerned. We do not have anywhere near two-thirds of the majority needed in either the House or the Senate for passage of the appropriate human life amendment. The only human life amendment that is adequate is one that will define pre-born children as human beings, as persons, who will then deserve the complete protection of the 14th Amendment. And we are tons of votes away from that.

Q: This last year saw for the first time the passage of the so-called Ashbrook Amendment, now sponsored by Rep. Chris Smith, banning the use of federal employee health insurance for abortion on demand. Didn't that represent a significant victory?

Mr. Brown: We have had some very significant victories, and I don't want to imply in any way that we're at a standstill. We can hold our own on funding legislation. In fact, I think we can make gains. But

as a movement, we have to be able to look down the road, not simply to next week or next month.

Q: Different pro-life approaches are favored by different members of Congress. Which do you favor and why?

Mrs. Brown: The most popular approach right now, favored by almost every single national organization in the pro-life movement, is the Respect Life Act, which was introduced in the Senate by Sen. Roger Jepsen, R-Iowa, and in the House by Rep. Henry Hyde, R-Ill. If passed, it would remove the government from promotion of abortion, funding of abortion and the provision of abortion as an alternative method of birth control.

In addition, the preamble of the bill clearly defines a pre-born child as a human being who exists from the moment of fertilization. Therefore, the United States Supreme Court is challenged in such a way that it would have to reopen the 1973 decision in Roe vs. Wade. We feel the Supreme Court would upon reflection possibly reverse itself. That is the main reason the pro-life movement is so excited over the Respect Life Act. However, again we're run into a situation in the House and in the Senate where there is little, if any, enthusiasm. That is because the political effort of the pro-life movement has been diluted, and a lot of the credibility of the pro-life movement has been diluted as well, due to the

factionalism which occurred last year over the so-called Hatch-Eagleton amendment.

We do not support any measure in Congress that will not restore personhood to the unborn child and that will not stop abortion.

Q: Has that factionalism been cured?

Mr. Brown: I think it's healing.

Q: Could you place the American Life Lobby in that movement? I've read that somebody called you the "Marine Corps of the pro-life movement."

Mrs. Brown: Nick Thimmesch, syndicated columnist for The Los Angeles Times, called us that, because since our beginning in 1979, we have never wavered in principle. We have grown extremely strong. We have more than 150,000 members. Our magazine goes into more than 100,000 households. One of the reasons why we have experienced such tremendous growth — especially in 1983 — is because we have never wavered from the very simplest principle upon which we became involved in the movement more than 12 years ago. If the pro-born child is a person, we have a valid fight. If the pro-born child is not a person, and we begin to compromise on his or her fate, even if it's only one baby, then we've lost the battle because we've lost our grassroots support.

The American Life Lobby has never wavered from the principle that each and every pre-born child is a human being, a child of God, deserving of equal protection under the law.

Q: Have you also been involved in some other pro-life activities — for example, you've taken some stands on the so-called Baby Jane Doe case. Can you relate that principle to the whole range of pro-life issues that you're interested in?

Mrs. Brown: The same principle applies. Baby Jane Doe is a person. Baby Jane Doe was born with problems. We feel strongly that she has civil rights, and that her civil rights need to be protected under the law. Simply because she is handicapped does not mean that the medical profession should be able to say that because her "quality of life" does not measure up to some nebulous standard — which none of us seem to be able to define — she does not deserve any surgery. From the moment that little girl was born, she was just as important to us — the American Life Lobby — as the millions of babies who had already been murdered.

The reason is she was on terminal, she has a problem. And we feel that it is incumbent upon our society to care for those children who have problems with equal protection the same way they would care for the healthy baby. We do not hold the decision of the parents against them. We would have had to turn to our doctors, and we would have had to have said, what is best for our daughter? Unfortunately, those parents asked that question from a team of doctors in New York who were willing to say her "quality of life" will never be adequate. Therefore, we recommend that you not give her proper medical attention. We disagree with that, and do not think that medicine should set those kinds of standards for the people of this country.

Q: Was there not also some disagreement about the extent of her disability?

Mr. Brown: What has come to light in the court documents themselves in certain conditions with regard to her very existence at birth were misrepresented to the press, and therefore, perpetuated by the press in error. For example, we read in the newspapers that her head was abnormally small. And yet in the medical records it is clear that for the sum of her entire form at birth as a person, her head was normal. The size of her head was never a problem. We were also led to believe that she would love in pain, even if she lived for 20 years. That is definitely not the case. Many physicians who have treated spina bifida children tell us that those babies do not suffer pain — depending on how quickly the surgery is performed, they can lead almost normal lives. And I use the word "normal" with great hesitation because it has become a word that can be bandied around by the medical profession. In her case, it has been used to deny her proper civil rights.

Q: One of the popular criticisms of the pro-life movement is the press is that while you don't want people to have abortions, you don't want to offer them any help otherwise.

Mr. Brown: I don't know how many times and of how many interviews I've given to the press that I have always somehow gotten around to the fact that there exist throughout the United States more than 4,000 organizations offering alternatives to abortion. These are very caring people who do a number of unique things. No. 1, they operate with no federal money whatsoever. It's all volunteer. They will take a pregnant woman into their home. They'll put her up. They'll feed her. They'll clothe her. They'll do everything to go through the birth with her. They will help her pay the child up for adoption.

If she chooses to keep the child, they'll find her clothes. They'll find her a job. They'll do everything. And if you look at the statistics on adoption itself, people wait from two to five years to find a child to adopt. So the pro-life movement is perhaps the most caring movement in America.

Article appearing in the Washington Times on January 20, 1984.

I pose with presidential candidate Ronald Reagan and Senator Paul Laxalt during a political gathering in early 1980.

> Wake up, and strengthen what remains before it dies. I find that the sum of your deeds is less than complete in the eyes of my God.
>
> I know your deeds; I know you are neither hot nor cold. How I wish you were one or the other—hot or cold! But because you are lukewarm, neither hot nor cold, I will spew you out of my mouth! (Rev. 3:2, 15, 16).

It was all too true. Clearly, I was headed straight for the condition of spiritual lukewarmness that is so hurtful to our Lord. I had become a couch potato in the vineyard of the Lord. That Lent I became acquainted, as never before, with my own need and my own faith—and with the need to nurture that faith with sincerity more than once a week on Sunday mornings.

It was a slow, painful process. It took almost a year to get down to my desired weight of 145 pounds. But with the Lord's help, I made it. I never went to a diet counselor or even a doctor. I just began taking vitamins, cooking for a family, and eating for a sparrow. What a novel experience, leaving food on the plate! When I stopped eating fat, the fat went away. Gradually I shrank from a size 24 to a size 10. My kids—now ages thirteen, eleven, and eight—really noticed the change. The day Hugh said to me,

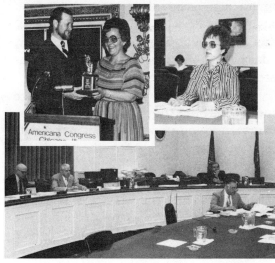

I accept Pro-Life Action League Award from League Director, Joe Scheidler, 1982. I testify against taxpayer funding for Planned Parenthood, as an apathetic Congressional Committee listens, 1983.

"Mom, you really look great!" was one of the brightest of my life.

The lawsuit that had started on Ash Wednesday ended, interestingly enough, on Good Friday, when our lawyer called to say that an amicable resolution had been reached. The fund-raising company took a hands-on approach to helping the Lobby retire a debt that had seemed unmanageable, and the Lobby, in turn, became a fiscally sound organization. Thus we turned a major corner in our ability to serve those who were looking for a pro-life group that would lead, not wait; that would fight, not stand still; that would hold the line for the babies, not cut deals.

Paul never wavered in his support of me through all this. People sometimes say that marriage is a 50-50 proposition, but they couldn't be more wrong. There have been times when our marriage was a 100-0 proposition, in one direction or the other. Through each of these periods our love grew stronger, our faith grew deeper, and our ability to withstand whatever was thrown in our way became greater.

It is impossible to continue in pro-life work without strong family support and constant re-examination of priorities. I always tell people that God gave me one vocation: to be a good wife and mother. When I falter in that vocation, then nothing else in my life will bear good fruit. To be pro-life is to be pro-family, and that commitment must take concrete, tangible form in the way we live our daily lives.

The events of this hectic year finally brought me to my knees—literally, at daily Mass. Receiving the Eucharist has become the cornerstone of my relationship with the Lord.

It humbles me that I had to sink so low before I could realize how distorted my priorities were, and how great my need for the Lord was. It was, of course, nothing more than what my parents had tried to teach me, what my grade school teachers had tried to model for me, and what the Lord himself had been trying to get across to me. It had taken an almost impossible set of crises to get the message through. But now the journey of faith had begun in earnest for me, and I believe it was this that made the coming events more spectacular for me than they would have been had I not travelled this road.

The Wilting
of the
White House

1983-1985

Do not grow lazy, but imitate those who, through faith and patience, are inheriting the promises.

Hebrews 6:12

Chapter Thirteen

MERICAN LIFE LEAGUE'S influence began to extend farther and farther. In late 1983 we helped sponsor an international pro-life congress in Rome. This gathering was the result of meetings throughout the previous year among pro-life leaders from various organizations, who agreed that the relationship of birth control to abortion needed to be addressed more strongly.

The congress was a real watershed. Speakers came to Rome from around the world—as far away as Africa and China—and told story after story of how officials from the United States Agency for International Development had vigorously advanced the pro-abortion, pro-death agenda in their countries. Tapes of these presentations were sent to officials in the Reagan Administration. We were certain they would make an impact there.

But no. We never heard a word from anyone in the administration about the tapes, the horror stories they contained, or the congress at which they had been recounted. The silence was deafening. Was our once-staunch White House starting to wilt? Was our pro-life president starting to reveal feet of clay?

Politics, we were to discover, could have strange effects on people.

1984 was an election year, of course. The year had long since been immortalized by George Orwell's famous novel—titled 1984—about a society where everything was turned upside down: weakness was strength, truth was fiction, black was white. And so it was that in 1984 we actually began to see pro-life dollars being donated to the reelection campaigns of several pro-abortion Senators. Why? Because they were Republicans, and it was considered important to retain a Republican majority in the Senate. No one ever seemed to stop and ask why a Republican majority was so important if the Republicans in question were not willing to support measures that would protect preborn babies.

1984 was also the year of a major international meeting in Mexico City. The meeting was to address the topic of world population. Policy-makers from governments around the world would be there. The aim of the meeting was to help disadvantaged nations address the economic problems caused by overpopulation.

It didn't take a genius to figure out what the agenda of many of those policy-makers would likely be: they would press for greater use of birth control and abortion, rather than addressing the real needs of families. We decided we needed a way to impact the meeting directly. We no longer felt we could trust the White House, where the "wilting" on pro-life issues was now almost complete.

So our staff personally collected and collated the material we thought the delegates ought to see, and sent a team to Mexico City to hand-deliver it. Former U.S. Senator James Buckley, a strong pro-lifer who was part of the U.S. delegation, helped us get the material into the right hands. It was also Mr. Buckley who announced, a few days later, that the United States would deny support to any government that used coercive family-planning methods, or that utilized abortion as a means of birth control. Mild as that policy was, it still sent shivers down the spine of the pro-death groups—which was precisely the intent!

1985 came, and with it the annual meeting of pro-life leaders with the president. That meeting changed my attitude toward politics, and politicians, forever.

The invitation for the meeting came via telephone, as was customary. In this case, the call came from the man who was the White House liaison for social policy affairs. The invitation was to both Paul and me—me because of A.L.L, Paul because of his political acumen and his experience with LAPAC.

In order to understand what happened, you need to know that these kinds of meetings with the president are always carefully prepared, almost scripted. Those invited to the meeting propose topics to be discussed, which are assembled into a briefing book. The president's staff review the contents of the book with him, so that he will be able to engage the issues without spending a lot of time on background information. The participants, for their part, decide ahead of time who will address which segment of the book, to avoid duplication of effort and to make sure all the main points get covered.

When the White House representative asked me which topic I wanted to address, I was able to respond immediately. We were facing a new threat, I told him: the entrance into our research centers of a drug called RU-486, which was designed to induce "do-it-yourself" abortions through the tenth week of pregnancy. It was imperative, I said, that federal funding of research on RU-486 be stopped, and that Food and Drug Administration approval of it be denied. I felt that the president could play an important role in this.

I was astonished by the man's response. RU-486 was not in the briefing book, he said. Therefore the president would not be prepared to discuss it fruitfully. Therefore I was not to bring it up at the meeting under any circumstances. After all, we did not want to embarrass the president.

Well, it seemed to Paul and me that if the president was unaware of what RU-486 was, and of the fact that his own government was sponsoring its development, then he needed to know about it, whether it was embarrassing or not. Most of the embarrassment, I suspected, would be on the part of those

Paul and me with Pres. Reagan, 1982.

To Judy and Paul Brown
With appreciation and best wishes, Sincerely,
Ronald Reagan

White House aides who seemed to be keeping the president in the dark on this crucial matter.

So when my turn came to speak at the meeting, I told President Reagan everything about the RU-486 "death pill." I handed him copies of research grants that the government was sponsoring, along with a book that had recently been released by those who supported the drug, and pleaded with him to stop the funding. He seemed amazed, though not particularly embarrassed. He asked me several questions and assured me that action would be forthcoming.

Paul, for his part, also launched into a topic that wasn't in "the book." He told the stories of several pro-life activists who had been given extraordinarily harsh jail sentences for a variety of alleged offenses. Couldn't the White House review these cases, he asked, and look into getting the sentences reduced or even remitted? The president said he was unaware that such cases existed, and promised to look into the matter.

History shows that the White House never did move to block the funding of research on RU-486, and did next to nothing about the pro-lifers who had been so unjustly treated by the courts. It was the clearest indication to date—as if any more indication were needed—of the wilting of the White House. For while President Reagan remained committed to a pro-life America, he was surrounded by staffers and advisors who either did not share his position or did not consider it a high priority. Indeed, we later learned that there were people in the administration who worked without ceasing to block action on any of the suggestions made during our brief meetings with the president. I—and perhaps most of the other leaders—was simply too naive to realize it at the time.

The only concrete result of that particular afternoon was that Paul and I were told we would never be invited back to the White House again. We felt vindicated, somehow. Had we acquiesced to the order to remain silent, had we gone along with the "briefing book game," we would have been untrue to our principles, to the babies, to our Lord. If we were going to offend someone, we decided, then White House staffers were the ones to offend, not the Lord.

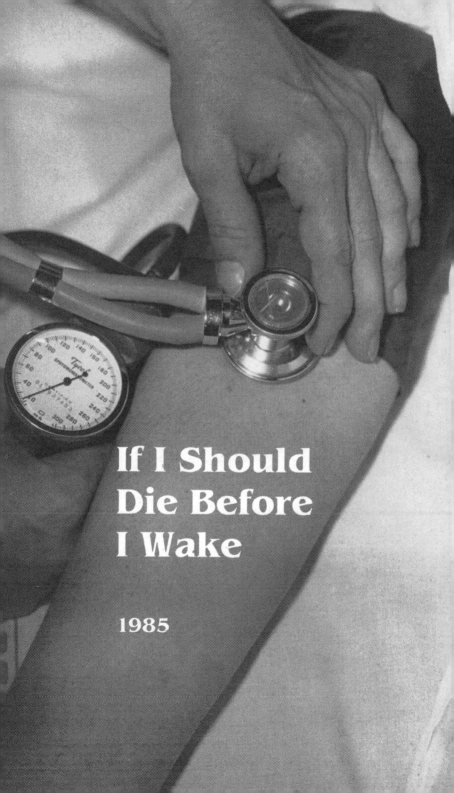

If I Should
Die Before
I Wake

1985

"Peace" is my
farewell to you, my
peace is my gift to
you; I do not give
it to you as the
world gives peace.
Do not be
distressed or
fearful.

John 14:27

Chapter Fourteen

HE YEAR 1985 was a year of some of A.L.L.'s greatest advances, and of one of the most harrowing crises of my life.

The nature of the pro-life struggle began to shift with the entry into the discussion of what were called "school-based clinics," or SBCs. The idea seemed simple, and innocent, enough: clinics located inside grammar schools, junior high schools, and senior high schools, where children could receive needed medical attention and counseling free of charge. Sounds great, doesn't it?

But we began to smell a rat when we saw the names of the people who were advocating SBCs. There was Douglas Kirby, a former official of the Centers for Disease Control (a federal agency) in Atlanta, who was a leading advocate of expanded sex education in the schools. He was also a proponent of providing birth control advice (and devices), as well as abortion referrals, either in the schools or in "clinics" located nearby.

There was also Joy Dryfoos, a researcher whose articles appeared regularly in Family Planning Perspectives, published by the Alan Guttmacher Institute, which is the research arm of Planned Parenthood. She became very vocal about the sad reality of rising teen pregnancy, which she attributed to a lack of adequate sex education in the schools.

Somehow, with people like this involved, we suspected that SBCs had an agenda beyond treating head colds and upset stomachs. And we were right: as the SBC movement picked up speed, it became clear that the primary purpose of the clinics was to advance the pro-birth control, pro-abortion agenda. There are documented cases of students going into such clinics for something as simple as an aspirin, only to be asked to complete a survey including intimate questions about sexual behavior. The follow-up to this, of course, is to offer birth control and abortion referral services to any students who might "need" them.

American Life League had produced many educational booklets about the relationship among birth control, promiscuity, and abortion, and had won the support of pro-life organizations from all church backgrounds. So when we went into battle against school-based clinics, we started with a solid reputation for our research and expertise. Many television and radio interviews and debates resulted. I've always been grateful to the Lord for the way we were able to spearhead what became a broad-based struggle to stop the spread of this new assault on our children.

1985 was also the year I was called upon to debate Faye Wattleton, the president of Planned Parenthood, on the Phil Donahue show. I was so nervous about the broadcast—the first one I had done "thin"—that I nearly became ill. I decided to go to Mass the morning of the show at St. Patrick's Cathedral in New York. I really wasn't concerned so much about embarrassing myself, but I didn't want to say anything that would contradict my faith and reliance on the Lord.

I took it as a sign of special favor from the Lord that Cardinal John O'Connor himself was the celebrant that morning. He was, and is, my hero. The point of his brief homily was that when we are in distress, we must give our problems to God with faith and hope. I knew this was the Lord's way of telling me not to worry. And indeed, the show went very well.

We debated RU-486. It was astonishing how candid and matter-of-fact Ms. Wattleton was in describing how the chemical could kill preborn babies through the tenth week of pregnancy, and how energetic the audience was in its appreciation of such efficient killing.

It seemed to me that Phil Donahue gave me more than my share of the time, perhaps hoping to balance things out a bit. Still, when I expressed support for chastity outside of marriage and fidelity in marriage, I thought Phil would have to have his jaw scraped off the floor. I felt utterly calm and at peace throughout the entire program. I knew the Holy Spirit was there, protecting me and guiding my tongue.

Then, in July, my world seemed to come crashing down around me.

It began with three days of hemorrhaging and a trip to the gynecologist. She gave me a D-and-C, then told me that her examination had indicated the presence of a possibly cancerous growth in my left ovary. A radical hysterectomy was necessary, she said, and the sooner the better. She referred me to a group of specialists at Georgetown University Hospital.

This was serious news indeed. There are many kinds of cancer, some more dangerous than others. Ovarian cancer can be one of the most dangerous of all. I went through a battery of tests at Georgetown, all of which confirmed the original diagnosis.

The doctors wanted to operate right away. There was only one problem: Paul and I had finally been able to plan a vacation together—the first one we'd had in many years—and we didn't want to miss out on it now. We planned to cover more than 3,000 miles driving, and to be gone about three weeks.

The doctor sat quietly for a moment, then said, "Go ahead. Three weeks won't make that much difference. Either it's already gone too far, or we've caught it in time, or we're just plain wrong about it being cancer in the first place. So don't worry, just have a good time." Paul and I looked at each other

Me with Father Paul Marx, O.S.B., at the Rome (PLAN) Conference, 1984.

and decided that we would have a good time. And we did. It was one of the most memorable and enjoyable trips we ever made.

The day before I went into the hospital, we invited a priest to come to the house for dinner. I had asked him to say Mass for our family, administer the sacrament of the Anointing of the Sick to me, and talk to the children about how to place their trust in the Lord. Naturally, it was very hard for the children—now ages sixteen, fourteen, and eleven—to face the fact that I might die. But it was something I wanted them to be able to deal with in a spiritual way. If I did leave them, I wanted them to have confidence that God had a perfect plan for me, and for them as well.

The next morning I said goodbye to Paul, in case I didn't get the chance to speak to him later, and assured him that everything would be okay. I learned later that while he sat in the waiting room during my surgery, he happened to pick up an article about the high number of women who die from ovarian cancer. It really tore him up. I was glad to have the opportunity to hear about it, and to be able to share with him my philosophy about death. How important it is to be spiritually prepared to die! How fortunate I felt to have had several weeks in which to make those preparations!

Me, recuperating at home after my surgery, 1985.

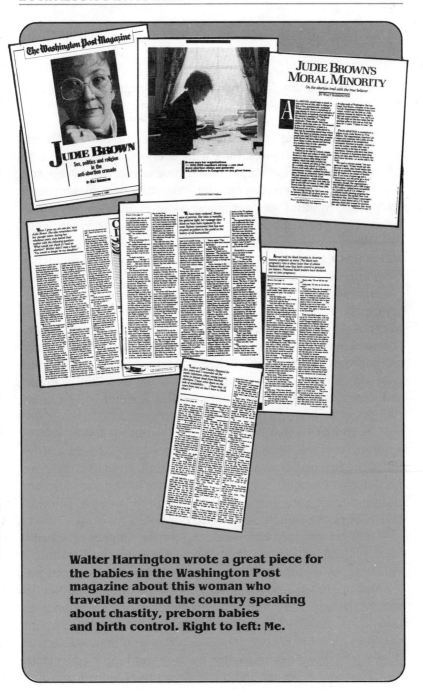

Walter Harrington wrote a great piece for the babies in the Washington Post magazine about this woman who travelled around the country speaking about chastity, preborn babies and birth control. Right to left: Me.

As things turned out, I did indeed have cancer cells in my ovary. Twenty-one separate biopsies were performed. But the operation was a success. All the cancerous cells were removed. I never needed any follow-up radiation or chemotherapy. To this day—praise God!—I remain cancer-free.

The doctor prescribed six full weeks of bed rest for my recuperation. I complied fully with everything he told me to do—not because I'm such a cooperative person by nature, but because Paul hovered over me like a mother hen, making sure I behaved myself! I was not allowed to get up from the couch for any but the most pressing reasons. You would have thought I was his child, not his wife. But that is the way Paul is—so warm and sincere in his love—and I am grateful to God for such a husband.

Still, we did occasionally have things to work out. I remember one Friday night about a week after the operation. Paul was going up to the high school to watch our son's football game. Then he told me he planned to have two women come over and baby-sit me! I begged and pleaded to be left alone. I promised to be a good girl and stay on the couch. In the end, Paul relented and cancelled the "baby-sitters." What a relief, to have an evening of peace and quiet, all to myself!

Six weeks to the day after the operation, I met with a reporter from the Washington Post who wanted to do a story about me for the paper's Sunday magazine. I had to chuckle at the timing. I thought, "Thank you, Lord, for loving me so much, and for allowing me to be used by you on this earth, whether it's for days or months or years to come."

Then on January 22, 1986, the paper arrived with a full-color picture of me on the cover of the magazine, and a wonderful story about this woman who travelled around the country speaking about chastity, preborn babies, and birth control. Though the writer, Walt Harrington, had the chance to flay me, he wrote a great piece for the babies. He wrote about pro-lifers in a positive way. I hope it affected him, and many of his readers, in some small way, so they can better appreciate the battle we are fighting and the sincerity of our efforts.

On the Field,
in the Courts,
at the Polls

1986 - 1988

Those who love your law have great peace, and for them there is no stumbling block.

Psalm 119:165

Chapter Fifteen

"**H**EY!" EXCLAIMS PAUL BROWN to Judie Brown. "Did you know that Tommy Herr is one of our donors? How about that? Tommy Herr!"

"Yeah, how about that," says Judie Brown to Paul Brown. "So who's Tommy Herr?"

So much for my knowledge of professional athletes.

Tommy Herr, it turned out, was the second-baseman for the St. Louis Cardinals at the time, renowned for his prowess both in the field and at the plate. It also turned out that he was pro-life, and that he liked American Life League enough to support us financially.

Learning that Tommy was one of our supporters immediately revitalized an old idea, that we start a group called "Athletes for Life." Another professional baseball player, Chris Speier, had tried to form such a group a few years before, but it had not gotten off the ground for a variety of reasons. Apparently the timing just hadn't been right in the Lord's plan.

But was the timing right now? One of our staff members contacted Tommy, who responded enthusiastically. Tommy so obviously loves the Lord and his word that he was perfect for the leadership role. As chairman of Athletes for Life, he was able to enroll many of his fellow ballplayers. He also appeared in a number of televised public service announcements, telling the American public the truth about the high failure rate of condoms, and that there was a foolproof way to prevent the transmission of AIDS through sexual contact: chastity. He was terrific.

The idea grew from there. Before long Mark Bavaro, the All-Pro tight end for the New York Giants, became co-chairman of Athletes for Life and started signing up professional football players as well. He even went to the first Operation Rescue event in New York City as an observer, and wound up in the paddy wagon. Athletes for Life has been extremely effective in carrying the pro-life message to the public, and especially to young people.

Speaking of Operation Rescue: I participated in a rescue that year as well. One of my favorite priests, Fr. James Buckley, told me he was going to participate and urged me to join him. So one Saturday morning I drove to Fairfax, Virginia, to join a group of rescuers bent on closing down a local abortion clinic.

It was an experience I'll never forget. We were all gathered on the sidewalk when the signal came to move into place in front of the clinic's doors. Everyone around me began moving. I had planned to join them. I lifted my right foot to take a step forward, and then simply got stuck. I can't explain it, but it felt as though my feet were literally riveted to the ground. I tried to move, but I absolutely could not do so. The rescue took place with me standing there, praying my Rosary, still frozen to the sidewalk.

There are many charisms and callings, as Cardinal O'Connor so frequently reminds us, and I was beginning to realize that perhaps participating in Operation Rescue was not one of mine!

Athletes for Life, begun in 1978, and carried forward in 1985 by American Life League, provides pro-life athletes with information and fellowship.

I applaud the valiant efforts of those who literally stand in the way of the slaughter, but it does not appear to be my calling.

A.L.L. was impacted by the rescue movement, though, in an unexpected and unwelcome way. In 1987, with Operation Rescue rolling across the country like a freight train, the abortion lobby came up with a new legal strategy: taking pro-lifers to court under a law designed to deal with organized crime. The law is called the RICO act, because of its stated goal of stopping Racketeer Influenced and Corrupt Organizations. The abortionists argued that Rescue's orchestrated attempts to close down abortion clinics violated this statute. And even though A.L.L. was not formally aligned with Operation Rescue, we were hit with a RICO lawsuit just the same.

It wasn't until 1989—after a lot of anxiety and a fortune in legal fees—that we were finally free of the case. Nothing really came of it except for a couple years of legal maneuvering. Yet the travesty of the RICO act continues. It is appalling that those

My one and only appearance on "Donahue" (Jan. 13, 1985) pitted me against Faye Wattleton, then President of Planned Parenthood; a physician; an audience; and Phil. The subject: Abortion Pill RU-486.

who kill babies are able to go about their business under the mantle of the law, while those who sacrifice so much to intervene on behalf of innocent preborn babies go to jail—as gangsters, no less!

I believe the history books will one day honor these courageous men and women who put their lives on the line for the sake of the babies, in an effort to awaken a slumbering nation to the horror of abortion.

I also believe that those who pray—for the preborn, for their mothers, and for their killers—are every bit as courageous, and every bit as effective, as those who intervene physically. Each of has our own gifting, and our own calling, from the Lord. He does not expect us to do what he has called others to do, only what he has called us to do. I believe he sees each and every aspect of pro-life work as his own love in action on behalf of the little ones. Whether or not we make the history books here on earth, we will all be included in the book our Lord is keeping!

As the 1988 presidential election rolled around, American Life Lobby received many letters from supporters, wondering how we planned to work for the Bush campaign and how they could join in. A lot of these people were angry—and more than a few stopped contributing—when we told them that we did not

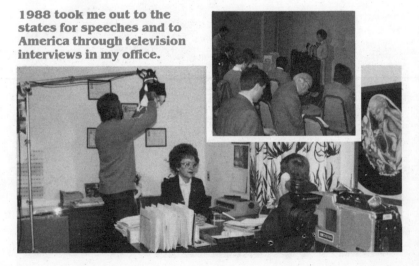

1988 took me out to the states for speeches and to America through television interviews in my office.

plan to do anything for the Bush campaign.

The reason was simple. Our board of directors, as well as all our legal and medical advisors, were unanimous in their conviction that protection of the child in the womb had to be absolute. As far as we were concerned, any candidate who wanted to wear the pro-life label had to be unequivocally committed to the principle that all the babies had to be protected, not just some of them. So when George Bush went on record as saying he opposed abortion except in cases of rape, incest, or to save the life of the mother, it was clear that we could not endorse him—even though his opponent, Michael Dukakis, was far worse.

The state of pro-life political action had been deteriorating for some time, and became especially troublesome in 1988. More and more candidates were trying to endear themselves to the pro-life movement by mouthing weak, equivocal statements. And more and more pro-life people were buying the argument that "something" was better than "nothing." The result was that the political clout of the pro-life movement had been severely diluted. A.L.L.'s position was clear and uncom-

1988 also took me to Congress to point out the plight of preborn children and their mothers as victims of abortion.

promising: we would give no political action committee endorsement to any candidate who did not stand four-square for the principle of personhood—for equal protection for all the babies.

The only bright spot of 1988 was Pat Robertson. He campaigned on the truth of what Planned Parenthood really stood for. He pointed out that the group's founder, Margaret Sanger, had been a racist. And he spoke forthrightly about how abortion was tearing at the heart of our nation. I believe strongly that if all pro-life leaders had put their full support behind Pat Robertson, we could at least have forced George Bush to adopt a more acceptable position. But it was not to be. Our movement failed to stand firm for the truth. Instead we built a stumbling block and fell over it ourselves.

Our opponents, of course, did not make this mistake. They did not give an inch to anyone. They wanted abortion-on-demand, right now, period. Their unbending insistence on the woman's "right" to "choose" easily overcame the pro-life movement's tepid stand of "no killing—except under certain circumstances."

Dr. Bernard Nathanson, former abortionist who later converted to the pro-life cause, points out that the pro-abortion forces have long been able to take advantage of compromise and disunity among pro-lifers. One of the main strategies of the National Abortion Rights Action League (NARAL), of which Dr. Nathanson was a founder, from its inception, was to stand solidly for its demands in the face of disunity and waffling from the churches and the pro-life groups. In particular, he said, it had taken advantage of disunity among the Roman Catholic hierarchy, working in various ways to drive the wedge in deeper.

It had worked as early as 1973, and it was still working in 1988. The pro-abortionists held fast to their cardinal principles while we shied away from our own. The tragedy of the "strategic," "something-is-better-than-nothing" approach is that babies die as a result. Would that we were more concerned with standing firm for God's truth than we are with finding acceptance in the halls of secular power!

EQUAL JUSTICE UNDER LAW

Matters
of Opinion

1989

I have come in my Father's name, yet you do not accept me. But let someone come in his own name and him you will accept. How can people like you believe, when you accept praise from one another yet do not seek the glory that comes from the One God?

John 5:37-38

Chapter Sixteen

CHRISTY WAS THE CENTER of my life during 1989. In most ways, the Brown family was doing great. Hugh was playing football at the University of Maryland—an experience that only the mother of a football player could possibly understand. Cathy had begun her studies at George Mason University. Paul's business had grown and prospered. His plant was now printing most of A.L.L.'s publications, and he himself was managing the organization's finances, so we could maximize the value of each and every penny donated by our 250,000 supporters.

The only cloud on the horizon was Christy. She was still at home. And she was ill. The problem was that no one could figure out the nature of her illness. She suffered severe chest and abdominal pain, which totally debilitated her every time it flared up. We went to doctor after doctor, who put Christy through test after test, only to come back shrugging their shoulders and shaking their heads.

Fortunately, A.L.L. now had a staff in place that did not require my physical presence in the office very much, as long as the telephone system kept operating, so I was able to stay home with Christy whenever she needed me. That was a great blessing, one for which I thanked the Lord often.

In the midst of our personal crisis with Christy, we began to face a dilemma on the pro-life front. It had to do with a Supreme Court case known as Webster v. Reproductive Health Services. It was one of the most closely watched abortion-related cases in many years.

A bit of background. William Webster was attorney general for the state of Missouri, whose restrictions on abortion were among the most stringent in the nation. Reproductive Health Services was a large abortion clinic in St. Louis. It had gone to court seeking to overturn the state's strict regulations. It is a legal convention that when you take a state to court, the case is listed under the name of the attorney general. Hence this particular case became known, for short, as the Webster case.

Webster offered a fairly straightforward choice between two basic points of view. One view held that states had the right to regulate abortion. The other held that no one could deprive a woman of her right to kill her preborn child. The decision, handed down on July 3, was a strong affirmation of the states' right to regulate abortion and thus a victory for the pro-life cause. But to turn an old saying around: this particular silver lining had a large, black cloud attached.

In its opinion, the Court said that state legislatures had the right to assert that human life begins at the point of fertilization if they believed that to be the case. This, in fact, was the basis on which the Missouri law was written. The Court did not say whether such a position was right or wrong, merely that states could assert it if they chose. Thus the Court adopted one of the wimpiest, trendiest positions imaginable—"it's true for you if you believe it"—and applied it to one of the most pressing issues imaginable: the definition of when human life begins. In effect, it made the personhood of the preborn child a matter of opinion—and of political horse-trading.

A.L.L. applauded the Webster decision as a step in the right direction. But not a very big step. It left unresolved the fundamental issue of personhood. Worse, it clouded this vital issue in the minds of many people, including many pro-life people. I had the opportunity to appear on the Oprah Winfrey show with Molly Yard, who was then president of the National Organization for Women, and make clear A.L.L.'s unswerving commitment to the personhood of all preborn children.

In August, American Life League held an educational seminar in St. Louis to discuss the Webster decision and where to go next in light of it. Brian Young of our staff had drafted ten different legislative proposals that could be advanced in state legislatures. Each of the proposals was in line with the provisions of Webster, meaning that it should hold up in court. Each one was based on affirming the principle of personhood. Each one offered legislators an opportunity to cripple the abortion industry, address the RU-486 problem, or provide new protection for the preborn child. More than 200 people attended. It was a great opportunity to discuss the issues, debate the proposals, and work toward a united position.

One group that did not attend—though they had been cordially invited—was the National Right to Life Committee. It turned out NRLC had its own legislative proposal, which it unveiled at a small conference in Washington, D.C., in October. Their proposal was based on extensive polling data, which indicated that while the vast majority of Americans were opposed to abortion as a means of birth control, many thought abortion should be permitted in cases of rape, incest, fetal deformity, and serious threat to the health of the mother. NRLC had drafted a legislative proposal embodying this poll data and planned to launch it in all fifty states.

I was disappointed with the NRLC proposal, for several reasons. The most obvious, of course, was that it failed utterly at the key point of the battle: by allowing for certain "exceptions," it undermined the principle of personhood, saying in effect that it was sometimes okay to kill babies.

I was also saddened that NRLC had chosen to bypass our August meeting and to unveil its proposal without inviting scrutiny from other groups and organizations. Once again, the pro-life movement was seen to be heading off in different directions. The press pounced on this disunity, weakening the strength of the overall movement. It also pounced on the NRLC's proposed exceptions to an outright ban on abortion, correctly seeing this as an accommodation of the pro-abortion forces.

For me, it was a sad turn of events. Had we simply given up on the principle of personhood? Were we really going to settle for protecting only some babies? Were we really going to be the ones to tell lawmakers which babies should be protected—and which babies were okay to kill?

I know, I know: compromise is the essence of politics, and pro-life political action is therefore bound to involve compromises. I accept this. I just think it is the politicians, not the pro-lifers, who should be doing the compromising. A legislator often goes into a battle knowing, and aiming for, what he most wants. Then, along the way, he may have to give up some of what he wants in order to get some of what he wants. That is the way Congress and state legislatures work.

But . . . it is one thing when a politician compromises on financing a new highway. It is quite another when he compromises on something that means the life or the death of innocent babies. Moreover, it is one thing when a politician compromises on an issue. It is quite another when the people committed to one side of that issue do the compromising for him. You can bet that lobbyists in other fields don't go to politicians and suggest ways in which their own interests can be undermined. Why, then, should we?

Suppose that after months of discussion and debate, a state legislator comes to A.L.L. and says, "Look, I know you want to stop all abortions. But I can only carry this bill right now if I allow for some exceptions. I'd rather get something than nothing." Our response is simply, "We will applaud whatever

In 1989, the Webster decision brought me face to face with Molly Yard, then President of N.O.W., on the Oprah Winfrey show.

gains you make. But we still won't be satisfied with anything less than a complete ban. After all, every abortion kills a human being. If you feel you have to compromise, that is your decision. But we won't compromise our principles."

That is very different than our walking into the legislator's office and saying, "Well, we'd really like to save all the babies. But it's okay with us if you let abortionists kill babies from the following categories. . . . " When we do this we make a mockery of our principles, and we undermine our own effectiveness as lobbyists. Politicians are already adept at compromising our principles: they don't need us to do it for them. That is why A.L.L. will always hold firmly to the absolute need to recognize and protect the personhood of each and every preborn child.

The crowning achievement of the year for A.L.L. was the completion of Champions for Life, a video starring six members of the 1987 Super Bowl Champion New York Giants. The video was made possible by the generosity of Mr. Wellington Mara, co-owner of the team. It was a tremendous success, something that could touch the hearts of young people in a new and exciting way. After all these years we finally had a tool to sway the teenager or college student who didn't want to buy the phony "pro-choice" arguments.

As the year drew to a close, I found myself praying more and more that we would not let ourselves be swayed either by the disappointments of politics and by our own human frailty, or by the fleeting pleasures of momentary success. It is so easy to get caught up in the excitement of a television appearance, an appointment with a prominent government leader, or an ovation at a speech.

Whether in the face of failure or success, we need humility. In less time than we like to think, we will be gone and our deeds—even our names!—forgotten. All that counts is whether we have faithfully done what our Lord has asked of us. He will never forget us.

Daddy had a major heart attack barely a week before Christmas. We had planned a traditional family Christmas at home—both Hugh and Cathy would be home from school—but those plans had to change. Because Christy was still suffering from her as-yet-undiagnosed illness, I decided to take her with me. Off we went to California.

The situation was worse than I had anticipated. Daddy's condition was quite serious, the doctors said. There was only one heart surgeon in the West who could perform the surgery he needed—and even then it was far from clear that Daddy would be strong enough to survive. The rest of the family flew out to join us. Daddy went into surgery on Christmas Eve.

I went to Mass and spent most of the day in the chapel praying. Tears streamed down my face as I gave my stepfather over to the Lord. I tried to pray simply that God's will be done. I knew it wasn't right to try to tell God what to do. But, I must confess, much of my praying probably sounded like precisely that.

Daddy survived the emergency quadruple-bypass surgery. But he was hanging on by a thread. The physician spoke with my sisters and me that night, and again on Christmas Day. He was not very encouraging. For days, Daddy lay in an intensive-care unit, hooked up to what seemed like dozens of monitors, machines, and feeding devices. If he did not show marked improvement soon, the doctor said, his chances of survival would become virtually nil.

Our prayers became increasingly urgent. Here lay a man, only sixty-four years old, who had given himself to our mother so unselfishly for so long, and who had poured himself out for us as well. The thought of losing him was more than we could bear.

Almost miraculously, it seemed, his condition began to improve. Within a few days he was unhooked from most of the machines. By the time we returned home he was smiling, happy, and in full control of the situation. His biggest concern was whether or not he would be allowed to drive his car.

None of us had ever received a better Christmas present. All we could say was, "Thank you, Lord, for loving Daddy, and for allowing us to have him with us a little while longer."

Betrayal
and Unity

1990

Justice will bring about peace; right will produce calm and security.

Isaiah 32:17

Chapter Seventeen

SOMETIMES THINGS happen where you least expect them. Who would have imagined that after years of conflict, debate, and activity in places like Washington, D.C., and New York, the pro-life controversy of the year would erupt in Idaho?

But that is exactly what happened. I suppose I shouldn't have been surprised. As I continued to attend daily Mass, I was becoming overwhelmed by the truth of the lessons I was reading in The Imitation of Christ, a spiritual classic that I think is "must" reading for everyone who is trying to serve the Lord. The closer I grew to the Lord in prayer and in the Eucharist, the more it became clear to me that those who follow him will share in his trials and sufferings. What happened in Idaho definitely fit the mold.

The model legislation prepared by the National Right to Life Committee—the one that would restrict abortion while making exceptions in cases of rape, incest, and so on—had been passed in the Idaho legislature and now lay on the desk of Governor Cecil Andrus, awaiting his signature. Governor Andrus was thought to be pro-life. He had said previously that he would sign a bill limiting abortion as long as it contained the familiar array of "exceptions." Now, such a bill lay before him. It needed only a stroke of his pen to become law.

But in the end, he failed. Rather than keep his word, he vetoed the very bill he had said would satisfy him. I can't say I was completely surprised. Betrayal is in the very nature of politicians. We pro-lifers had been led on, and then let down, many times before. But there were many angry, broken-hearted people left in the wake of the governor's deceptive tactics.

Our American Life League affiliate in Idaho was angry with

the Idaho legislature. One of A.L.L.'s pieces of model legislation had been put forward for consideration, but had been passed over without a second glance. Our bill would have at least forced some debate on the fundamental principle of personhood for all unborn children. Given the governor's subsequent actions, it is unlikely it would have passed. But as it was, the legislature simply opted for the NRLC proposal, laden as it was with exceptions, and the principle of personhood never even got discussed.

Moreover, the pro-life movement in Idaho was badly split by the whole affair. Some had supported the NRLC bill. Others had insisted on the need to provoke discussion of personhood. In the end, neither camp got what it wanted. I have often wondered why all the pro-life groups didn't sit down together right at the beginning and work through their differences before any bill was introduced. Maybe together they could have seen through the governor's hypocrisy in calling for a bill he later refused to sign.

All in all, the Idaho fiasco represented the tragic waste of a

Unity 90 featured more than 60 speakers, including (clockwise) Congressman Henry J. Hyde (R-IL); John Cardinal O'Connor with me; Mildred F. Jefferson, M.D., President, Right To Life Crusade; and Csaba Vedlik, Lobbyist, American Life Lobby.

golden opportunity to force the bedrock issue of personhood into the light of day.

As it happened, the Idaho veto came at almost the precise moment we were finally discovering the cause of our daughter Christy's pain. We had been to more than a dozen doctors over the course of more than a year. Christy had become so weak that she couldn't even go to school; I was teaching her at home. So when her latest doctor explained that she had an enlarged colon—about three times normal size—and said he wanted to perform surgery to pare it down to size, we consulted two other doctors for corroborating diagnoses, and then agreed to the operation. Christy was in the hospital for less than a week. Four weeks after the operation she celebrated her sixteenth birthday, and she has been fine ever since.

A.L.L.'s major event of the year was the pro-life show of shows, called "Unity 90." We hosted a four-day conference in Chicago with representatives from virtually every major pro-life organization. We also broadcast a three-hour video conference that was beamed to more than 250 locations across North America and was seen by millions of people. It was so wonderful, I can only urge you to get the video and see it for yourself.

Judge Bork was there—the one so cruelly abused by the Senate during his Supreme Court confirmation hearings—along with other major pro-life leaders, such as Cardinal O'Connor of New York, Dr. Jerry Falwell, Dr. Mildred Jefferson—

1990: Mr. and Mrs. Bart Gaffney of New York visit me at our offices; I visit Senator Jesse Helms to present him with a gift for him and his wife, Dot.

my old mentor from the early days at NRLC—Dr. Bernard Nathanson, and many others.

And for three hours of the evening of Saturday, June 30, Americans got the chance to see how respectable, how caring, and how dedicated the pro-life movement is. There were compelling guest appearances by Chicago Bears football coach Mike Ditka and rape victim Kay Zibolsky. Rev. Wilbur Lane, eighty-eight years old and completely blind, received our "Hero of the Year" award.

When the dust settled and the mail began to pour in, we learned that Unity 90 had helped spur the formation of several new pro-life groups, including one for policemen called Officers for Life; had played a direct role in saving the lives of at least three babies; had re-invigorated many pro-lifers suffering discouragement after many years "in the trenches"; and had given witness to the reality of pro-lifers being committed to God first of all, and then to the rights of the innocent, whether in the womb or in the nursery, whether in good health or bad, without exception.

Unity 90 was a great success. And it nearly destroyed us! After it was over, we went into a financial tailspin. I kept telling people it was all part of God's plan; that he wouldn't have brought us this far down the road just to shove us over a cliff!

And indeed the trials and tribulations did work out to our ultimate benefit. For the first time in our history, a group of businessmen came forward and offered to form a "kitchen cabinet," a group of advisors who could guide us out of our current quandary and help us with our financial decisions in the future. These men, who are still with us today, are like a crown of precious jewels on the head of the pro-life movement. The rest of us have been so busy fighting the fight that we have never really learned about budgets, cash-flow statements, and the other things that credible organizations are made of. We deeply appreciate the gift of their time and expertise—and trust it is but the beginning of a groundswell of corporate support of the pro-life movement.

The Future
Is Ours

What I tell you in the dark, speak in the daylight; what is whispered in your ear, proclaim from the roofs.

Matthew 10:27

Chapter Eighteen

THE HISTORY OF THE pro-life movement—your history and mine—continues to be written. As we look to the future, there are some difficult realities we must deal with. It is better to do this sooner than later, so that we can be mentally and spiritually prepared for the challenges that lie ahead.

First let's take a look at the Supreme Court. Some recent decisions may help us see which way the Court is headed.

Many pro-lifers did not notice the Court's decision in the 1991 Johnson Controls case. In this case, the Court ruled that a company may not take special precautions to protect its female employees from hazardous chemicals, since to do so would be to discriminate against them on the basis of sex. This was specifically applied even to women who are pregnant or who may desire to become pregnant in the future.

The Court decided this case unanimously, which means that not even one Justice looked beyond the feminist agenda to consider the possibility that the life of a preborn child might be worth protecting. The Court considered only the career aspirations of the mother. No thought whatever was given to the rights of the preborn baby. Once again, the Court simply refused to acknowledge the personhood of the preborn child.

As vacancies on the Court have arisen in recent years, much speculation has focused on whether enough votes exist to overturn Roe v. Wade. Naturally, I hope this vicious ruling will be overturned, and the sooner the better. But overturning Roe will not, in itself, put an end to the killing: it will only send the question back to the states, where it was before. As long as the justices refuse even to address the fundamental issue of personhood, no meaningful protection of the preborn is going to come from the Supreme Court.

What about Congress? As I write these words, there are fewer reliable pro-life votes in the House and Senate than at any time since the early 1980s. There may be enough votes to sustain a presidential veto on bills that would use tax dollars to fund abortion. But for a thoroughly pro-life bill, one providing genuine protection for babies in the womb, we would not be able to muster a simple majority in either house. Indeed, there may be fewer than thirty pro-life votes in the entire United States Senate.

What about the state legislatures? In 1991, more than 200 pro-life bills were proposed and discussed. Only a dozen actually passed. And of these, not one would provide a suitable test case for the Supreme Court either to overturn Roe or to consider the issue of personhood.

The media, of course, continue to mislead the public with solidly pro-abortion rhetoric. In 1991 the Supreme Court actually handed down a pro-life decision, holding in Rust v. Sullivan that government had a right to say whether tax dollars could be used to pay for the promotion and referral of abortion. The pro-abortion forces claimed that this ruling "gagged" them. It did no such thing, of course. They are still free to promote killing all they want: they just can't use your tax dollars—or mine—to do it. But the media focused exclusively on the so-called "gag" effect.

Seems like a pretty grim picture, doesn't it? Well, there's only one thing to do: redouble our efforts to turn things around! Worrying about past failures won't help. Crying over missed opportunities won't help. Whining about lack of resources and volunteers won't help. We need to put our shoulder to the wheel and start changing the situation. Right now. Right where we are. Today.

What should you do? Why not let the Lord tell you? Pray sincerely and ask him how he wants to use you. I do not know what the Lord wants of you. But I do know that you can find out if you ask him. Perhaps our greatest need as a movement is for more prayer, more fasting, more earnest seeking of God's perfect will.

Let me tell you what American Life League is doing to carry on its tradition of leadership in the pro-life arena. We remain, as always, committed to protecting all preborn children, as well as their mothers and fathers and all those whose right to life is threatened.

First, we are committed to countering the extraordinary media bias that essentially denies pro-life people a forum for their views equal to those who espouse the pro-death ethic. Since we cannot depend on the media to tell our story accurately and fairly, we are pursuing three outstanding communications projects.

The first is **Celebrate Life! television.** American Life League's thirty-minute program is already on the air in many locations, and its impact is being felt. We focus on ordinary people doing extraordinary things, constantly bringing new faces into the spotlight. This is the first time in the history of the pro-life movement that a weekly television program has carried our message into millions of homes without censorship or media bias.

If you believe your community could benefit from this program, but cannot find it on any of your local broadcast or cable stations, write to me (the address is in the back of this book). I'll tell you how you can go about getting it on the air, how

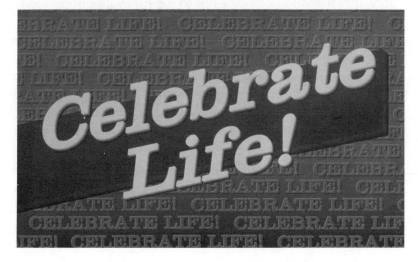

to get videotapes of programs that have already aired, and how to start educating your community by means of this program.

Next is **Celebrate Life! radio.** American Life League produces a two-minute update, five days a week, on what is happening in the pro-life battle and how people like you can get involved in the crucial work of saving babies' lives. Again, if you'd like to help get this up-to-date, concise, educational program on the air in your area, write to me.

The third project is what we call the **Truth Squad.** We began this project in 1991 as a way to monitor coverage of pro-life topics in local newspapers—like yours—around the country. It works like this: when someone sees something in the paper that is clearly inaccurate, distorted, or biased, they notify A.L.L. We, in turn, either respond to the paper ourselves or prepare a suggested course of action for the local individual or group.

We also make available a reprint of a series of articles by David Shaw, an investigative reporter for the Los Angeles Times, that help make clear how biased the print media can be. Many groups have found it very productive to show these articles to their local editor, along with samples of biased local coverage.

Both the Truth Squad and the reprint materials are remarkably effective and helpful. Write to me for more information.

Dealing with the press, and with the general public through radio and television, is worthwhile, you say. But what about my neighbor, my classmate, my co-worker? How can I prepare myself to share the pro-life message with him or her?

Here are three tools A.L.L. can send straight to your home to help you:

1. ALL About Issues, American Life League's acclaimed magazine, is filled with educational helps, true stories, and access to other resources that can help you, your family, and your group make a difference for the babies. It gives you confidence in discussing difficult topics and late-breaking events, knowing that what you have to say is reliable and accurate.

2. VOICE, our new magazine by and for young Americans, ages fourteen to twenty-two. This bi-monthly is packed with helpful material for young people who want to take a stand. It covers chastity, alternatives to abortion, the horrors of Post-Abortion Stress Syndrome, and other vital topics.

3. communique, a handy, four-page newsletter that comes out every two weeks. I put a lot of time into this publication, which features concise reports on pro-life-related developments in medicine, social policy, politics, and the activities of

pro-death organizations coast-to-coast. If you need a quick, easy-to-use resource for timely news, action items, and resource referrals, write to me and ask to receive communique.

All the resources and materials I have mentioned so far are produced by American Life League, the premier educational organization in the United States today.

In late 1991, because of our continued strong emphasis on education as the key to victory, the Board of Directors of American Life Lobby determined that it was in the best interest of our many supporters and our pro-life friends to discontinue the "Lobby" as a separate organization. New IRS regulations for educational groups like American Life League have made it possible for one organization to carry on the work that was formerly accomplished by the Lobby while continuing to emphasize education and outreach.

Throughout the past 24 years, our family has grown in spirituality, maturity, and dedication to the preborn, their mothers and their fathers. We love each other very much, and here we are in January, 1992, enjoying precious time together— the five Browns: Paul, Judie, Hugh, Cathy and Christy.

Precious resources can now be used by one organization, American Life League, to accomplish the goals that have been set forth in this book and in the League's Mission Statement. The 1990s demand this of us—careful stewardship combined with continued leadership placing us on the cutting edge of the effort to restore respect for all innocent human life.

A.L.L. and I are committed to seeing the day—in the not-too-distant future—when the killing will end, when the innocent and defenseless will be protected, and when our hard-earned tax dollars are no longer being spent to peddle death and the destruction of the family. We want to see a strong, vigorous, united pro-life movement, with an effective presence in every town, every city, and every state in our nation. We are committed to helping each and every person who is on our side so that one day America will just say no to abortion, and the killing will stop at last. Write to us. We can help you make a difference.

Paul and I face the future deeply committed to stopping the killing of innocent babies through increased education.

Afterword

Wherever I have come from, I am still going forth. Wherever I have been, I hope I have made a difference. Whatever I have done, it has really been the Lord working through me, since by myself I can do nothing.

Mother Teresa has said that she is nothing but a pencil in the hand of God. Oh, that I might be such an instrument!

I have laid my life before you, not to draw attention to myself, but in the hope that seeing how God has worked through another ordinary person will motivate you to turn to the Lord and ask, "Lord, what would you have me do?"

I began writing this book at my stepfather's house early in 1991. I had travelled to Southern California to be with him because he had suffered another major heart attack, from which he almost died. Each month I returned to spend a few days with him. My husband, Paul, and our children have been so gracious in allowing me the freedom to go. They know how much I cherish Daddy.

Daddy finally recovered his strength, and in October of 1991 he, along with his seventy-two-year-old brother Kenneth, drove across country to visit my family in Virginia! God is so good.

When I look at Daddy, still alive after so many crises . . . when I look at the miracles the Lord has done in my own life. . . when I think of what miracles he is able to do in your life as well . . . I know that one day the killing will stop. Our Lord is too merciful, and too powerful, for it to be otherwise.

But he has chosen to do his work through us, and he gives us only what we ask him for. Have we yielded ourselves to his power and purpose as fully as we should? Have we pleaded with him as earnestly as we should for an end to the slaughter? For forgiveness of our country for the grave sin of abortion? For a renewal of our own commitment to his lordship in our lives? Have we thanked him lately for loving us more than we could ever imagine?

Why not do it right now? Tomorrow may be too late.

About Issues

Educating thousands

Inspiring activism

Touching the hearts of mothers and fathers

Providing accurate and well-researched material

The premier magazine of the world-wide pro-life movement

$**24**^{95} **per year, and a subscription can be yours**

RESOURCES

American Life League produces a weekly 30-minute television program focusing on the theme: ordinary people do extraordinary things – **CELEBRATE LIFE!**

Copies of each program become available on VHS videotape once the program has aired, and each program on VHS is available for a cost of **$10.00**.

In addition, American Life League publishes more than 80 separate resource items that can be used to combat the evils of abortion, euthanasia, permissive sex instruction, family abuse and more.

Please complete the coupon below to receive a full listing of these valuable resources, along with an order blank for your convenience.

And should you require specific information about any of the work American Life League is doing, please let us know by using the coupon below.

Clip and
Mail to:

Educational Resources
P.O. Box 1350
Stafford, VA 22554

Please send the resource catalogue and order blank.

Please send me more information about the following:

_____

PLEASE PRINT:

Name _____

Address _____

City _____ State _____ Zip _____

Phone # (_____) _____